George Walter Chamberlain

Soldiers of the American Revolution of Lebanon

George Walter Chamberlain

Soldiers of the American Revolution of Lebanon

ISBN/EAN: 9783337236144

Printed in Europe, USA, Canada, Australia, Japan

Cover: Foto ©Suzi / pixelio.de

More available books at **www.hansebooks.com**

SOLDIERS

OF THE

AMERICAN REVOLUTION,

OF

LEBANON, MAINE.

By

GEORGE WALTER CHAMBERLAIN, B. S.,

Member of the Maine Historical Society.

---

*" The dead do not need us, but forever and for-
evermore we need them." —James A. Garfield.*

Weymouth, Mass.
Weymouth & Braintree Publishing Co.,
1897.

Introduction.

Lebanon, Maine, is the birthplace of the writer of the following pages. Four generations of his ancestors lived, died, and are buried in its soil. The two older generations lie in unmarked and unknown graves. What is true of the writer's ancestors in Lebanon is also true of three-fourths of those buried in Lebanon previous to 1820.

Of the two or three hundred graves in the First Parish Cemetery, there are to-day only about twenty-five having stones properly inscribed, the earliest bearing the date, 1805.

To rescue from oblivion the names of those early settlers of my native town who rendered military service to the United States in maintaining American Independence is the chief reason for these pages. Their names and military services deserve to be perpetuated by succeeding generations.

No Lebanon Revolutionary soldier's name or service has been omitted intentionally ; and yet, it is doubtful if *all* Lebanon men who were in the service between 1775 and 1783 have been found and are included in these pages. The war rolls of New Hampshire and Massachusetts in all probability do not contain a complete list of names.

Considerable difference exists in the nature and length of these sketches. This difference arises, not from any desire to magnify nor minify any record, but from a great difference in the amount of material that came under my eye when searching for facts relating to Lebanon heroes of the Revolution. Each man's sketch is the story of the records.

My grateful acknowledgement is due to many, and, especially, to Hon. Samuel Wingate Jones, M. D., a life-long friend and neighbor, who, in his ninetieth year, with memory unimpaired and historic interest undiminished, has read my manuscript with care and given invaluable suggestions and criticisms.

G. W. C.

West Lebanon, Maine, 31 July, 1896.

ABBREVIATIONS USED :—b. for born; bapt., baptized; Co., Company; Col., Colonel; d., died; g. s., gravestone; L., Lebanon; m., married; pub., publishment; Reg't, Regiment.

SOLDIERS OF THE AMERICAN REVOLUTION

OF

LEBANON, MAINE.

BERRY.

1. THOMAS BERRY was living in L. as early as 1774, when on 6 Jan. he hauled wood for the Rev. Isaac Hasey. Mr. Hasey wrote a bond for him 6 Aug., 1774. In Mr. Hasey's diary for 1775 he wrote on 18 May: "Tom Berry assisted" in farm work. In Mass. Archives, Vol. 19, p. 161, he is described as "a private, belonging to the town of Lebanon, in Capt. Jedediah Goodwin's Co. of Col. Edward Wigglesworth's Reg't; discharged at Albany, N. Y., 30 Nov., 1776." He was one of the men of whom Mr. Hasey wrote 22 July, 1776, "our Men with Lieut. Cowel Set out for Canada."

He probably resided in town temporarily, as the name is not found on the church, parish, or town records. It is found in Mr. Hasey's diaries only.

BLAISDELL.

2. JOHN BLAISDELL was b. Aug. 15, 1756. The Rev. Amos Main of Rochester, N. H., entered on the records of the First Church of Rochester the following: "1757—At ye Ministers Fast at Towow [Lebanon] Baptized Jn.º Blaisdell", etc.

He enlisted as a private in Capt. Samuel Grant's Co. of Col. Oliver Titcomb's Reg't and received pay for two months' service and for travelling *to* and *from* Rhode Island 18 July, 1777. He also enlisted 10 Nov., 1777, as private in Capt. Oliver Titcomb's Co. of Col. Jacob Gerrish's Reg't, and after nine days' service was promoted to Sergeant of the Guards raised for guarding prisoners after the surrender of Burgoyne's army. He served until 2 April, 1778. He was made a Mass. state pensioner for life 5 Feb., 1816.

He m. (1) at L. 12 July, 1779, Abigail, daug. of John and Sarah Legro, the first of that name to settle in town. He m. (2) 24 March, 1822, Mrs. Sarah (Blaisdell) Horne, widow of Richard Horne of L., and daug. of Enoch and Sarah (McIntire) Blaisdell of L. She was bapt. at L. 3 July, 1777.

John Blaisdell was ordained a Free Baptist clergyman at Lebanon 21 Nov., 1799, by Benjamin Randall, the founder of that denomination. He was the first permanent resident Free Baptist clergyman in L. He continued to preach in this and adjoining towns until his death 30 Aug., 1823. He settled the farm now (1896) owned by Amasa Grant, in the year 1779, which farm is situated in the northwesterly part of the town not over one-half mile from the Milton, N. H. line. By his wife Abigail, b. 5 Aug. 1762, he had:

   i. THANKFUL, m. Benjamin Dixon of L.
   ii. RACHEL, b. 1782; m. Joseph, s. of Joseph and Alice (Farnham) Burrows of L.; she d. 15 Nov., 1837, ae. 55 years.
   iii. SALLY, m. Rev. David Blaisdell of L.; he died 23 July, 1842.
   iv. ABIGAIL, b. 3 March, 1786, m. Rev. Roger Copp; she died in 1853 or '4.
   v. JOHN, JR. b. 29 Jan., 1790; m. 23 May, 1819, Betsey, daug. of Benjamin and Betsey (Churchwell) Gerrish of L.; he d. 3 March, 1836.
   vi. SAMUEL, b. 10 May, 1792; m. Hannah, daug. of Gershom Lord of L.
   vii. DOROTHY, b. 20 Oct., 1794; m. Daniel, son of Elisha and Mercy (Tibbetts) James of L.
   viii. RUTH, b. 23 April, 1797; m. Jacob, s. of Reuben and Ruth (Lord) Goodwin of L.
   ix. ALICE (ELSIE), b. 5 May, 1799; m. 3 Nov., 1832, her cousin, Samuel Blaisdell of Rome, Me.
   x. URIAH, b. 9 May, 1803; m. Eliza, daug. of Jonathan and Mary (Churchwell) Copp of Ossipee, N. H.; resided in Somersworth, N. H.
   xi. ELIZA, b. 6 March, 1807; m. Oct., 1833, her cousin, Thomas Blaisdell of Rome, Me.
   xii. MARTHA, m. Solomon Seymour; resided in Portsmouth, N. H.

BURROWS.

3. DAVID BURROWS of L. was the son of Deacon Edward and Mary Burrows, who were original settlers of L. He was born about 1760, and was baptized 23 March, 1766, by the Rev. Isaac Hasey, first settled pastor of the First Parish of Lebanon. He enlisted in the Revolutionary army for three years at Berwick, Me., 20 Dec., 1781. He is described on the muster roll of Dominicus Goodwin as of "light complexion, five feet, eight inches in stature, and twenty-one years of age."

He was stationed at West Point where he died in about four months from the time of his enlistment and before 16 April, 1782. He was probably in Capt. Bowman's Company of the 5th Massachusetts Regiment. His brother, Jonathan Burrows, who was in Capt. Bowman's Company at that time, wrote from West Point on 16 April, 1782, to "Deacon Edward Burrows, Living in Lebanon, County of Old York," "the terrifying news of David's death." He had, however, no opportunity to forward the letter, now on file in the Pension Department at Washington, until 21 May—thirty-five days after its composition.

4. JONATHAN BURROWS of Lebanon was a son of Dea. Edward and
Mary Burrows of L. He was born about 1753, and had reached his
majority just before the beginning of the Revolution. He enlisted
three times. On 20 May, 1775, he enlisted in Capt. Philip Hubbard's Co., of Col. James Scammon's Reg't, which regiment was stationed on Bunker Hill, while the battle of the Seventeenth of June
following occurred on Breed's Hill. Scammon's Reg't was not in the
battle on that day, however.

His second enlistment, for three years, was before 10 March, 1776,
on which day he was a recruiting officer at Berwick, Maine, where
Jonathan Knox of Berwick and others enlisted under him. He soon
marched to Boston and joined Capt. Sullivan's Co. of Col. Joseph Cilley's Reg't and Gen. Enoch Poor's Brigade He then marched
to New York with his troops from which point they sailed to Albany,
thence marching to Montreal.

During these three years he served for a portion of the time as
First or Orderly Sergeant. In February, 1777, he was in Capt.
Amos Emerson's Co. of Col. Joseph Cilley's New Hampshire Reg't.
Col. Cilley's report sent from Valley Forge 10 Jan. 1778, describes
him as "Serg't Jonaⁿ *Burris*, at time of his enlistment 23 years of
age, five feet, eight inches in height, eyes, hair and complexion light,
left at Manchester because of sickness." He was then in Capt.
Amos Emerson's Co. of the First New Hampshire Regiment. On
another roll he is described as "Jonᵗ Burroughs, Serg't, Fifth Co.,
First Reg't, commanded by Col? Joseph Cilley."

In 1781 (probably 20 Dec.) he enlisted again for three years in
the Continental service, joining Capt. Bowman's Co. of the Fifth
Massachusetts Regiment. This time he served fourteen months and
27 March, 1783, secured a substitute in Joseph Stephens (Stevens)
of Lebanon who voluntarily consented to serve the remaining
twenty-two months for the wages due on account of Burrows from
15 Jan., 1782, to 15 April, 1783. Writing to his father after his
brother David's death, he said, "I am left alone and entirely com-
fortless." At this time, 21 May, 1782, he had living in Lebanon a
young wife and child, which fact connected with his brother David's
death explains why he wrote from West Point on the 16 April, 1782,
as follows : "Times are very dubious at present, for there is no
news of peace as yet. The Armies are all well disciplined and in
wonderful[ly] good spirits, and draw very good provisions, but no
money. *Since my misfortune has been so great*, I should be very
glad to be free from the service, but do not know how to get clear."
* * * * * *

He, with four other brothers and one sister, was baptized at Lebanon 23 March, 1766, by the Rev. Isaac Hasey, first settled pastor
of the First Parish of Lebanon. In his letter to his father already
referred to, there is evidence that he possessed deep religious convic-
tions. On 25 May, 1780, he married at Lebanon, Elizabeth, daughter of Thomas and Elizabeth Witherell, who were original settlers of
Lebanon. At the close of his term of service in the Revolution, he
returned to Lebanon, where he ever after resided. He was a select-

man of the town for 1784, 1786, and 1787. For many years he resided on the Witherell-Burrows farm, long since abandoned. On this farm is the old family burying lot, in a neglected spot, covered with shrubbery and surrounded with tall poplars that are destined to perpetuate the local name of the neighborhood, "Poplar Hill." The stones in the burying lot are shamefully shattered, giving evidence of having been used for targets by ruthless sportsmen. From the fragments of one can be read :

"LIEUT. JONATHAN BURROWS,
died Jany 2, 1817, aged 64 years."

As his widow, Elizabeth Burrows lived in Lebanon many years, receiving a pension from the Federal government, and in 1838, a grant of land from the State. She died at Lebanon 23 Dec. 1850, "aged 90 years and four months," (g. s.) and was buried by the side of her husband whom she had joined in holy wedlock seventy years before. Their children were :

i. THOMAS WITHERELL, bapt. 7 Oct., 1781; killed in battle in the Second War with Great Britain.
ii. DAVID, bapt. 22 June, 1783; m. at Lebanon 27 Dec., 1804, Polly Wentworth; died 2 Nov., 1823 (?)
iii. NELLY, bapt. 26 Sept., 1784; m. at Lebanon 22 Nov., 1804, Thomas Goodwin, Jr., son of Thomas and Anna (Hodgdon) Goodwin of Lebanon.
iv. GILES WILLIAM, bapt. 9 Dec., 1784; m. at Lebanon 6 May, 1810, Polly Furbush; captain of town militia; merchant; died at L. 11 Oct., 1822, in the 36th year of his age. (g. s.)
v. INFANT, d. 6 June, 1786. (g. s.)
vi. ELIZABETH, bapt. 20 June, 1790; m. at L. 29 Nov., 1810, David Farnham, Jr. (See 24.)
vii. EUNICE TWOMBLY, bapt. 15 July, 1792; m. at L. 9 Oct., 1814, Isaiah, son of Thomas and Eunice (Knox) Legro of L.
viii. JONATHAN, JR., bapt. 4 Oct., 1795; m. at L. 28 July, 1821, Abigail, daug. of Thomas and Anna (Hodgdon) Goodwin of L.
ix. JAMES, bapt. 16 Sept., 1798; resided in Massachusetts.
x. ASENATH, bapt. 27 June, 1801; m. John Lord of L.
One child d. 24 May, 1809. (g. s.)

CANNEY (KENNEY).

5. JOHN CANNEY (Kenney), b. at Dover, N. H., 24 Aug., 1744, was a son of Samuel and Susannah Canney of Dover, N. H., and Lebanon. The father, Samuel, removed from Dover, N. H., to Lebanon about 1747, where he became the *first settler* within the township. The son, John Canney, enlisted as a private in Capt. Jedediah Goodwin's Co. of Col. Edward Wigglesworth's Reg't. He was in the same company of which Ichabod Cowell was lieutenant, and "Parson" Hasey's diary shows that on "22 July, 1776, our men [Lebanon men] with Lieut. Cowell set out for Canada." His discharge was dated at Albany 30 Nov., 1776.

As a selectman he rendered services in 1770, 1771, 1772 and in 1780, 1781, 1782. He removed from the original Canney farm now (1896) owned and occupied by David W. Varney to the farm now (1896) owned and occupied by Samuel Shapleigh. He was engaged in farming and lumbering until his death which occurred about 1799.

He was buried in the "Camp Hill" Cemetery, but the inscription on his supposed stone is unintelligible. In 1782 he was chosen lieutenant of the town militia and a little later Colonel, by which title he was called.

He m. Mrs. Elizabeth (Thompson) McCrillis, the widow of Daniel McCrillis of Lebanon. She had no children by Canney, and lived to be 96 years of age. Her children by Daniel McCrillis were: Robert (59); John, who m. 25 Nov., 1765, Mary Garland; Elizabeth, who m. 25 Oct., 1768, Daniel Roberts; and Jane, who m. Richard, son of Benjamin and Hannah Furbish of L.

CHAMBERLAIN.

6. JASON CHAMBERLAIN (William[4], William[3], Jacob[2], William[1]) a native of Rochester, N. H., but a resident of Lebanon, Maine, and of Wolfboro', N. H., was a son of Capt. William and Eleanor (Horne) Chamberlain of Rochester, N. H., and Lebanon, Maine.

He was born at Rochester, N. H., probably on the original Chamberlain farm, which was at "Willow Brook," on the westerly side of the main road leading from "Haven's Hill" to "Norway Plains," so called, 9 Feb., 1756. When young he learned the tailor's trade, probably of Mr. John Roberts, Sr., who followed that trade, and lived on the Haven's Hill Road in Rochester, at that time.

On a muster roll dated 13 June, 1775, Jason Chamberlain "of Rochester," "a private," occupation a "taylor," aged "19 years," is described. He was then in Capt. Jonathan Wentworth's Co., of Col. Enoch Poor's New Hampshire Reg't. Capt. Wentworth's Co. was composed chiefly of men from Somersworth and Rochester in New Hampshire, and from Berwick and Lebanon in Maine.

Mr. Chamberlain, with others of his company, acknowledged receiving "pay for coats promised his company, 12 Oct., 1775." He enlisted a second time as a volunteer and received therefor a bounty of ten pounds at Rochester 10 Aug., 1778. This enlistment was in Capt. John Hill's Co. of Col. Joshua Wingate's Reg't., dating from 7 Aug., 1778. He "turned out" to join the Continental Army at Providence, Rhode Island, under Gen. Sullivan, and was discharged after 28 days of service.

He returned to Rochester where 2 Feb., 1780, he was married by the Rev. Joseph Haven, then pastor of the Cong'l Church, to Mary, daughter of Daniel and Abiah Brewster of Rochester.

Early in 1783, with his father's family, he removed to the adjoining town of Lebanon, Maine, where he resided on part of the farm now (1895) owned by the heirs of Charles Burnham Chamberlain. While living in Lebanon he was engaged in tailoring going from house to house, when needed, after the custom of that time.

On 26 Feb., 1790, Mr. Chamberlain removed from Lebanon to Wolfborough, N. H., where he resided until near the close of his life. In 1820 he is reported as a Revolutionary pensioner, but only for a short time, as he died in Jan., 1823, and is buried at Tuftonborough Neck, N. H. His wife, Mary, died in March, 1830 or '31.

Jason and Mary (Brewster) Chamberlain's children were: Daniel, William, Jason, Jr., Abiah, Mary, Eleanor, and one who died in childhood. From the six who married and had children, there are many descendants who have become widely scattered.

CLARK.

7. JOSIAH CLARK, a native of Berwick, or Wells, Me., is named on a list of six months' men raised by the town of Wells, Me., to serve in 1780. He is described on the roll, Mass. Archives, as 38 years of age; 5 ft., 10 in. in stature; of ruddy complexion; a resident of Wells. He arrived at Springfield, Mass., 4 Aug., 1780, in the 33d Division under command of Capt. Samuel Carr. He marched 20 July, 1780, and was discharged 7 Sept., following.

He m. at Berwick, Me., 13 Feb., 1776, Patience, daug. of Ebenezer and Martha (Wentworth) Hanson of Berwick. After the Revolution he removed to the farm in Lebanon now (1896) owned and occupied by the heirs of Francis A. Shapleigh. He was living in town 25 Aug., 1782. His wife was baptized and joined Hasey's Church 16 Aug., 1807. He d. at Lebanon in 1834; she was a pensioner, and died at Lebanon in Feb., 1848, at the age of 92 years. (Town Records.) Children:

  i. MARTHA, b. Oct., 1777; m. at L. 15 Jan., 1804, Tobias Smith of L.
  ii. ABIGAIL, m. at L. 26 Aug., 1804, George Nichols of L.
  iii. EBENEZER, m. at L. 29 Oct. 1807, Sally, daug. of Ichabod Smith of L. He removed to Rome, Me.
  iv. PATIENCE, m. Ephraim, son of Ephraim Tebbetts. He removed to Belgrade, Me.
  v. MARY, m. at L. 22 Nov., 1814, Paul Stevens of Acton, Me.
  vi. MERCY, m. at L. 6 Sept., 1814, John Cowell, brother to Ichabod who m. Rebecca Clark.
  vii. REBECCA, m. at L. 22 Dec., 1811, Ichabod Cowell, brother to John.
  viii. EUNICE, m. Jesse Waldron. (?)
  ix. ELIZABETH, bapt. 16 Aug., 1807; m. Mark, son of Samuel and Amy (Kilgore) Cowell of L.; resided in Somersworth, N. H.
  x. JONATHAN, bapt. 16 Aug., 1807; m. Rebecca, dau. of George and —— (Kenneston) Fall of L.; resided in L.

COLE.

8. EBENEZER COLE, probably a native of Somersworth, N. H.; resided there in early life. He removed to Lebanon as early as 1773, where he resided until he enlisted in the Revolution. He was a private in Lieut. Thomas Bragdon's Co., stationed at Kittery Point, Me., 5 Nov., 1775. He was in the service three or more times. The Rev. Isaac Hasey recorded in his diary, 11 Aug., 1776: "Bill up by Mrs. Cole for her husband in ye army;" and 18 Aug. again: "Bill up by Mrs. Cole for her husband sick in ye army." The "Parson" wrote 9 Nov., 1776, "Bill up by E. Cole for his *son* returned from ye army."

Between 30 May and 13 June, 1777,, he enlisted in Capt. Samuel Derby's Co. of Col. John Bailey's Battalion, and his name was reported with others mustered by Joseph Bragdon on a muster-roll, dated "York, 13 June, 1777."

On 14 March, 1778, Hasey recorded, "Bill by Mrs. Cole for her husband in ye army;" and on *15 May he wrote, "Cole died in ye army." He was at Valley Forge 25 Jan., 1778. (See Mass. Archives, Vol. 10, p. 81.)

His wife was Mary (Molly) daughter of Ebenezer and Sarah (Roberts) Wentworth of Somersworth, N. H. She was born about 1744, and became a member of Hasey's Church 11 July, 1773.

Mr. Cole resided on a part of the farm now (1896) owned by the heirs of Benjamin C. Hurd; and a section of this farm called the "Cole Field" perpetuates the name of this hero who gave his life for our American Independence.

His children, baptized at Lebanon 20 Aug., 1773, were Abigail, Esther, Mary and Sarah Wentworth; 25 Sept., 1774, Ebenezer, Jr.; and 21 Dec, 1777, Ruth. After Mr. Cole's death, his widow married a second time according to the Wentworth Genealogy, which also mentions another daughter by Cole, named Phebe.

He either had a son in the army in 1776, or his father was the E. Cole referred to by Mr. Hasey.

COOK.

9. ABRAHAM COOK, born at Rochester, N. H., about 1761, is described on the muster-roll as of "dark complexion, five feet, five inches in stature." He enlisted at Portsmouth, N. H., Nov. 1779, at the age of 18 years; and served on board the United States ship "Ranger," Thomas Simpson, captain, Elijah Hall, lieutenant. The "Ranger" sailed from Portsmouth to Boston, and from Boston she put to sea in company with the "Warren" and the "Queen of France." After some time they captured a small British privateer, and on the day following, encountered the "Georgia Fleet" so called. This fleet was under convoy and these American vessels took nine or eleven of the fleet. The prizes were taken to Boston, and then to Portsmouth, N. H., where Cook, with others, was discharged after five months of service as a marine.

In the Mass. Archives, Vol. 45, p. 282, he is mentioned as in the Second Reg't, 13th Co., engaged to reinforce the Continental Army for nine months, agreeable to a resolve of the General Court of the State of Mass. Bay, passed 9 June, 1779; and in Vol. 29, p. 116 of same, he is mentioned as in the First Mass. Reg't serving to Jan'y 1, 1781.

In the spring of 1781 he enlisted at Lebanon to serve for three years, or during the war; marched to Boston; joined the First Mass. Reg't. in Capt. Allen's Co. as a private; was at West Point and served two years.

At the close of the war he returned to Lebanon, and soon married Sarah Nutter of Newington, N. H. When the Second

---

*War roll reads "17 May, 1778."

War with Gt. Britain occurred, he enlisted again, but this time never to return. While in the service he died at Greenbush, L. I. (?) 15 July, 1813, leaving a widow, who was living as his widow 1 June, 1840 at the age of 84, and a large family.

His widow received a grant of land from the State under the resolve of 17 March, 1835, which grant was lot No. 4, or 5, in the First Range of lots in the township of Mars Hill, Me. She deeded her lot to David Legro of Lebanon who bequeathed it to Hon. Samuel W. Jones, M. D., of Lebanon.

When the line between Maine and New Brunswick was established by the terms of the Webster-Ashburton Treaty of 1842, a part of this land fell to New Brunswick. In recent years the United States government indemnified the owners who lost their possessions at Mars Hill in 1842.

"Cook's Hill" in the southerly part of the town of Lebanon where Abraham Cook resided perpetuates his name. I have been unable to find any family record.

10. DANIEL COOK of Lebanon enlisted as a private in Capt. Ebenezer Sullivan's Co. of Col. James Scammon's Reg't. 5 May 1775. He served three months and three days. Col. Scammon's Reg't was at Bunker Hill on the memorable 17 June 1775; but Frothingham states that his men were not in the actual battle of that day. (Mass. Archives, vol. 16 p. 44.) On 5 Jan., 1779, the Rev. Isaac Hasey records the marriage of Daniel Cook Junr. and Christian Perry at Lebanon. I have found nothing more on Lebanon records concerning any Daniel Cook.

11. DAVID COOK enlisted 5 May, 1775, in Capt. Eben'r Sullivan's Co. of the Thirteenth Reg't. of Foot commanded by Col. James Scammon and belonging to the United Colonies of North America.

He m. at Lebanon 19 July, 1772, Abigail Garland, daug. of Dodavah Garland of Lebanon, the Rev. Isaac Hasey performing the ceremony. He died in the army, and his widow Abigail m. second, at Lebanon 13, or 18, May or June, 1779, Richard Perkins (64) of Lebanon, "Parson" Hasey again performing the marriage.

COPP.

12. SAMUEL COPP, one of the early settlers of Lebanon, came probably from the adjoining town of Rochester, N. H., as early as 1767. He settled in the extreme western part of the town, in the Salmon Falls river valley, and was the first person to clear a farm in that immediate locality. The house erected by him in 1778, the oldest now (1896) standing in town, is owned and occupied by Frederic Dixon, being in a good state of preservation.

On 14 July, 1776, Rev. Isaac Hasey wrote in his diary: "Bill up by Sam. Copp for himself bound into ye army"; and on the next day he wrote, "Col. Goodwin here to muster and pay men."

On a New Hampshire muster-roll dated at Charlestown, Mass., 27 July, 1776, his name appears as a lieutenant in Capt. Drew's Co., raised for Canada out of Col. Evans's and Col. Badger's Regts. Capt. Drew was of Barrington, N. H.

20 Nov., 1776, at Mount Independence, he, with other army officers, signed a petition for certain persons for field-officers in the third Battalion.

He was the first representative to the General Court from Lebanon, in 1772 ; a selectman of the town in 1777 and 1778 ; a member of the First Church from 20 Aug., 1780 ; a deacon from 1781, and subsequently an elder in that church. He was a man of great physical strength, as were his sons. He was buried on the farm that he cleared, and his grave, unmarked, is in what is now a pasture on the hill-side of the Dixon farm. "Copp's Bridge," spanning the Salmon Falls river near this farm, is all that the present generation have to remind them of Samuel Copp. His first wife was Hannah Hayes of Rochester, N. H., by whom he had ten children. He married second, at Lebanon 21 June, 1798, Sarah [(Scates) Knox-Wentworth] widow of Thomas Knox of Berwick, Me., and of Nathaniel Wentworth of Middleton, N. H. He died before 1818 at which date his widow Sally paid a ministerial tax. Children by wife Hannah, not arranged according to ages :

i. JANE, bapt. 28 Sept., 1780; m. at L. 5 Jan., 1786, Joseph White, son of John and Elizabeth (Cole) White of L.; resided in Ossipee, N. H.
ii. REUBEN HULL, bapt. 28 Sept., 1780; m. at L. 11 April, 1788, Eleanor Rugg; resided in L. He d. while on a visit in Chandlersville, Me., 2 Sept., 1840, æ. 75 y., 6 m., 24 d.; she d. 27 June, 1837, æ. 69 y., 7 m., 22 d.
iii. SAMUEL, JR., bapt. 28 Sept., 1780; m. at L. 21 Aug., 1794, Margaret Rugg; removed to Central Maine.
iv. SARAH, bapt. 28 Sept, 1780; m at L. 31 Dec., 1801, Joshua, s. of Thomas and Anna (Hodgdon) Goodwin; resided in L.
v. DOBAVAH, bapt. 28 Sept., 1780; removed to Wakefield, N. H.
vi. HANNAH, bapt. same time ; m. pub. 10 Nov., 1806, to Elijah Ricker of L.
vii. GEORGE, bapt. same time; m. 8 Nov. 1798, Sally, daug. of Thomas and Anna (Hodgdon) Goodwin.
viii. JONATHAN, bapt. same time ; m. at L. 4 Feb, 1802, Mary Churchwell; resided in Ossipee, N. H.
ix. ROGER, b. 21 May, 1781; bapt. 22 July, 1781; m. (1) 2 Aug., 1802, Mary Lord; m. pub. (2) 24 March, 1810, to Abigail, daug. of Rev. John and Abigail (Legro) Blaisdell of L.; an active member of First Free Baptist Church as early as 1812; ordained a Free Baptist clergyman in 1822; resided in town until 1834, when he removed to Chandlersville (now Detroit) Me., where he continued to preach until his death which occurred after 1853.
x. BENJAMIN HAYES, bapt. 7 Sept., 1783; m. at L. 29 June, 1806, Hannah, daug. of Samuel and Sarah (Hodgdon) Goodwin of L.; resided on east side of the Copp homestead, and later removed to Central Maine.

CORSON (COURSON.)

13. AARON CORSON (Courson) came to L. from Rochester, N. H., about 1769. His brother Samuel Corson came to this town

about 1760 and d. in 1785. Aaron was a Corporal in Capt. Jedediah Goodwin's Co. of Col. Edward Wigglesworth's Reg't. The roll shows that he was discharged at Albany, N. Y., 30 Nov., 1776.

He was an original settler of the farm now (1896) owned and occupied by the widow of William A. Corson. He was buried in "Camp Hill" Cemetery in an unmarked grave.

He had a son John Sr. who m. at L. 13 Nov., 1794 Tamson Hodgdon; he d. 18 April 1855 ae. 82 years (g.s.); she died 10 July 1865, ae. 91 yrs. 1 mo. 16 ds. (g.s.).

He had another son Enoch who m. Betsey daug. of Daniel and Dorothy (Tuttle) Lord of L. His daughter Dorcas, died unmarried.

14. JOHN CORSON (Courson) of Lebanon enlisted 20 May, 1775 in Capt. Philip Hubbard's Co. of Col. James Scammon's Reg't. Scammon's Reg't. of Maine men was on Bunker Hill while the battle of 17 June, 1775, occurred on Breed's Hill. Corson was a private and died in the army 27 July, 1775. His parentage I have been unable to learn.

15. MOSES CORSON (Courson) of Lebanon m. at L. 15 May, 1769, Elizabeth Perkins, the Rev. Isaac Hasey performing the marriage.

He enlisted (See Mass. Archives, Vol. 56, p. 196,) in Capt. Philip Hubbard's Co. of Col. James Scammon's Reg't. Scammon's Reg't. composed of Maine men, was at Bunker Hill 17 June, 1775, and witnessed the memorable battle of that day. On 18 May, 1775 Rev. Isaac Hasey wrote in his diary, "Mose Corson sowed and harrowed ½ bushel of peas" [for me]. On 18 June 1775 Mr. Hasey wrote, "Bill up by Elizabeth Corson for her husband in ye Army;" and 2 July, 1775 he again wrote, "Moses Corson Came from ye Army."

COWELL.

16. ICHABOD COWELL was b. 25 Dec. 1734. (g. s.) He is first mentioned at Rochester, N. H., where the Rev. Amos Main as a physician charged him for medical attendance 18 Sept., 1756. At a town meeting held at Rochester in 1762 he was chosen field-driver.

He removed to L. soon after 1762 where he became an original settler in the First Division of Home-Lots. The farm he first cleared is now (1896) owned by Warren Jones of Rochester, N. H.

He was twice in the Revolutionary army. In Capt. David Copp's Co. mustered by Capt. George Turner 25 Nov., 1775, he was No. 45. This company of "minutemen" was raised pursuant to an order of the Committee of Safety given 12 Oct., 1775, and a portion of the men went to Winter Hill, Charlestown, (now Somerville) to take the place of the retiring Conn. troops in Dec. following.

On 22 July, 1776, he enlisted at Berwick, Me., as a lieutenant in Capt. Jedediah Goodwin's Co. of Col. Edward Wigglesworth's

Reg't. from which he was discharged at Albany, N. Y., 30 Nov., 1776.

The Rev. Isaac Hasey wrote in his diary on Sunday 21 July, 1776 : "Bill up by Ichabod Cowell for himself and son [John] going into ye army." On the day following the "Parson" records : "Rode to Cocheco, and Berwick where lo[d]ged at Col. [Jedediah] Goodwin's ; our men with Lieut. Cowell set out for Canada."

His farm in the First Division he sold, presumably to Col. John Goodwin who was its owner in 1782. After his return from the army he removed to the Second Division where he purchased and cleared "Lower Lot No. 7." "Parson" Hasey recorded that his house was raised 4 Oct., 1788. On this lot now (1896) owned and occupied by Isaac Chamberlain he established the first grocery store in the western part of the town.

He was chosen a selectman in 1769, 1770, 1773, 1774, 1779, and 1785. He joined the First Parish church of L. 11 July, 1773, and on the same day his sons were baptized. His wife, the mother of these children, bore the given name Priscilla. He d. at L. 9 Jan. 1823 (g. s.) and was buried in the family lot of David Legro.

During the Revolution Legro was his waiter in the army and the friendship there formed become so strong that "Squire" Legro frequently invited his *master* to his own home. While on a visit Lieut. Cowell was taken ill and died at Legro's. He was buried in the Legro lot, at the foot of Gerrish's Hill. There the *master* and the *servant*—heroes of the Revolution—lie side by side.

Issue by wife Priscilla :

17.   i. John, bapt 11 July, 1773 ; enlisted as private 22 July, 1776, at Berwick, Me., in Capt. Jedediah Goodwin's Co. of Col. Edward Wigglesworth's Reg't. ; set out with his father for Canada ; discharged at Albany, N. Y., 30 Nov., 1776 ; m. at L. 1 Dec., 1783, Martha Kilgore.

   ii. Samuel, bapt. 11 July, 1773 ; m. at L. 14 April 1787, Amy Kilgore ; resided in the northerly part of the town ; "Cowell's Mountain" perpetuates his name.

   iii. Edmund, bapt. 11 July, 1773 ; b. 1 Nov., 1766 ; m. at L. 1 Jan., 1787, Comfort, dang. of Samuel and Molly Corson of L. ; he d. 24 Nov., 1850, æ. 84 y., 24 d. (g. s.) ; she d. 25 Jan., 1856, æ. 89 y., 9 m. (g. s.) He was an active member of the First Free Baptist Church of L. into which he was bapt. 1 Aug., 1804 ; his house was raised 30 Sept., 1788 ; he was for ten years a selectman in 1813, '14, '16, '17, '19, and from 1821 to 1824, inclusive ; he resided on the lot now (1896) owned by the heirs of Levi Cowell, who was a grandson ; his sons were *Isaac*, a merchant, *Edmund Clark*, a farmer, and *David Blaisdell*, a Free Baptist clergyman, born 20 Dec., 1806, and who died 15 April, 1884. (g. s.)

DOOR (DORE, DORR).

18. Beniah Door (Dore, Dorr,) of Lebanon, and of Milton, N. H., was a son of John and Charity (Wentworth) Door, early settlers of Lebanon. He was born at Lebanon about 1765 ; enlisted as a private 9 July, 1780, in Capt. Timothy Emerson's Co. of Col. Thomas Bartlett's Reg't, raised in New Hampshire to join the Con-

tinental Army for the defence of West Point. He was discharged 20 Oct. 1780.

He enlisted again, in 1781, from Lebanon for three years; marched to Boston; then to West Point where he joined the army; was in Capt. John Fuller's Co. of Col. Sheppard's Fourth Mass. Reg't.; the war closed and he was discharged before his term expired.

He resided in Milton, N. H., many years and was living there in 1838, a Revolutionary pensioner under the law of 18 March, 1818. He had a son Richard who lived in Acton, Me. He m. at Berwick, 1 Oct. 1786 Experience Andrews of Berwick.

19. JOHN DOOR of Lebanon, either the son of Philip and Sarah Door of Rochester, N. H., or the son of John and Charity (Wentworth) Door of Lebanon. He was either father, or brother, to Beniah and Jonathan Door, as both were named John, and were living in Lebanon in 1776.

John, the Revolutionary soldier, enlisted as a private 24 Sept., 1776, in Capt. Abraham Perkins's Co. of Col. Pierce Long's Reg't., stationed at New Castle, N. H. He served until 7 Jan'y, 1777, and received advanced pay from 7 Jan'y, to 7 Feb., 1777; but refused to march to Ticonderoga with his company, claiming that he belonged to Mass. and not to New Hampshire.

He was No. 41 on 24 Sept.; later No. 39, then 42; and from 7 Jan'y, to 7 Feb., 1777, he was No. 30 of his company. John Door Sr. lived at South Lebanon on the farm now (1896) owned by the heirs of Moses E. Varney.

20. JONATHAN DOOR of Lebanon, and of Milton, N. H., was a son of John and Charity (Wentworth) Door of Lebanon where he was born about 1759.

He enlisted in Capt. Caleb Hodgdon's Co. 9 July, 1776. This company was commanded by Capt. Abraham Perkins after 19 Sept., and it belonged to Col. Pierce Long's Reg't, stationed at New Castle, N. H. Mr. Door served until 7 Jan'y, 1777 when he received advanced pay for one month at Portsmouth, N. H.; but refused to march to Ticonderoga with his company, claiming that as he was a citizen of Mass., he was *not* under the laws of New Hampshire. He was discharged for refusing to march, and again enlisted in May 1777 as a private in Capt. Samuel Grant's Co. of Col. Titcomb's Reg't. He served two months and 18 July, 1777 received pay for services and travelling *to* and *from* Rhode Island.

When, on 9 Aug., 1777 the General Court issued a draft for able bodied, effective men, the towns of Lebanon and Kittery (including Eliot) furnished one company of 52 men with Elisha Shapleigh as captain, and Jonathan Doore as lieutenant. Mr. Hasey wrote on 19 Aug., 1777, * * * "every Sixth Man Draughted to go to war."

Again the Mass. Archives, vol. 37, p. 108, shows his name as private, belonging to Lebanon, in Capt. John Goodwin's Co. "in a

detachment of militia from the County of York under command of
Major Daniel Littlefield on an expedition to Penobscott, in compliance with a resolve of the Council of Mass. passed June ye 29,
1779." On this expedition Mr. Door travelled 210 miles.

In the autumn of 1779 he enlisted on board the "Ranger;"
sailed from Portsmouth to Boston; from Boston the "Ranger" in
company with the "Warren" and the "Queen of France" put to sea;
sometime later they took a British privateer; and on the day following, came in contact with the "Georgia Fleet." It was under
convoy and they took nine or eleven sail of the "Fleet." They returned to Boston and then to Portsmouth where Door was discharged
after a service of five months. He served as a marine on the
"Ranger," Thomas Simpson, commander.

His last enlistment was as a private 9 July, 1780, in Capt.
Timothy Emerson's Co. of Col. Thomas Bartlett's Reg't. raised in
New Hampshire to join the Continental Army for the defence of
West Point. He was discharged 26 Oct., 1780.

He returned to Lebanon where on 24 Aug., 1786 he was united
in marriage with Rebecca Garland by "Parson" Hasey. In 1786 or
1787 he removed to Milton, N. H., (then Rochester) where he was
residing in 1838 at the age of 79 years.

21. PHILIP DOOR, son of Philip and Lydia (Mason) Door of
Rochester, N. H., Lebanon and Shapleigh, Me., enlisted 22 July,
1776, as a private in Capt. Jedediah Goodwin's Co., of Col. Edward
Wigglesworth's Reg't.

On 22 July, 1776, he "set out for Canada," as Hasey says, and
was discharged at Albany, N. Y., 30 Nov., 1776. On 8 Sept., 1776,
"Parson" Hasey wrote in his diary : "Bill up by Molly Door for her
husband in ye army."

He was married at Lebanon 1 June, 1769, to Mary, daughter of
James and Mercy (Foss) Locke of Barnstead, N. H. The First
Parish records contain the following baptisms of their children :

i.   SIMON, bapt. 10 Oct., 1773.
ii. HANNAH, bapt. same time.
iii. JOSEPH, bapt. 21 May, 1775.
iv. MERCY LOCKE, bapt. 2 Nov., 1777.
v.   EDWARD LOCKE, bapt. 22 Sept., 1782.
vi. JAMES, bapt. same time.

22. RICHARD DOOR was either the son of Philip and Lydia (Mason) Door of Rochester, N. H., or the son of Richard and Patience
(Tebbetts) Door of Lebanon. From data at hand I cannot deter-
mine whether he was the father Richard, or the son Richard living in
Lebanon in 1776.

Richard, the soldier, enlisted as a private 3 Sept., 1776, in Capt.
John Brewster's Co. of Col. Pierce Long's Reg't, stationed at New
Castle, N. H. He was in the service 95 days.

FALL.

23. GEORGE FALL of Lebanon, a son of Betsey Fall, who removed to Lebanon in 1760, was born about 1755. He enlisted from the towns of Wakefield and Somersworth, N. H. On 7 March, 1775, he went to Wakefield, where he was employed to work for Samuel Hall until Nov.

He first enlisted as a private in Capt. David Copp's Co., Nov. 5, 1775, and was first stationed at Pierce's Island. His company of "minutemen" was raised by order of the Committee of Safety, issued 12 Oct., 1775; and a part went to Winter Hill, Charlestown (now Somerville) in Dec. to take the place of the retiring Conn. troops. His mother declared, 27 Sept., 1781, that he went from the Island to Cambridge where he enlisted in Capt. [Jonathan?] Wentworth's Co. for one year.

He enlisted at Somersworth, N. H., 12 March, 1777, in Capt. James Carr's Co. of Col. Enoch Poor's Reg't. On another muster-roll he is described as of Wakefield, N. H., enlisting for three years in Capt. Carr's Co. of the Tenth Reg't of New Hampshire Militia, commanded by Col. Joseph Badger, in a return dated 19 June, 1777.

He was a Sergeant in Capt. Carr's Co., and at one time he was attached to the Second Reg't of the New Hampshire line under Col. Enoch Poor; later under Col. George Reid. In March, 1781, he returned to L., having served more than three years. In his affidavit he states that he served continually until 6 June, 1783, when he received his discharge bearing the signature of General Washington. He was a pensioner from 3 Aug., 1829, until his death. (Land Office Files No. 144, Augusta, Me.)

He resided in the northerly part of the town on the "Durrell place," and was buried in the field now (1896) owned by Frank Lord. His grave is unmarked.

He m. (1) —— Kenniston; m. (2) widow Dorcas Kenney of Ossipee, N. H. The following imperfect family record is submitted. Children by *first* wife :—

    i. IVORY, m. Lydia, daug. of Noah and Keziah (Brackett) Lord of L.
    ii. *GEORGE, JR., b. 12 Nov., 1791; m. pub. 24 Sept. 1814, to Mary, daug. of Gershom Lord; she b. 24 April, 1791. George, Jr., was selectman of L. in 1831, 1832 and 1833.
    iii. MARY (Polly) m. Daniel. bapt. 9 July, 1801, son of Thomas and Anna (Hodgdon) Goodwin; resided in L.
    iv. ANNA, m. Nathan, Jr., s. of Nathan and Mercy (Knox-Downs) Lord; resided in L. and Somersworth, N. H.
    v. JAMES, removed from town to Lynn, Mass., where he resided.
    vi. JOHN, a blacksmith, went to Mass., but returned to L.; joined First Church 11 Feb., 1824.
    vii. MERCY, b. 1791; m. Benjamin, son of Nathan and Mercy (Knox-Downs) Lord; resided in L.; d. 6 Feb., 1867, æ. 76 yrs., 2 mos. (g. s.)

---

*NOTE—The Wentworth Genealogy gives George Fall, Jr.'s marriage 10 April, 1819, to Tamson, daughter of Benjamin and Rachel (Stimpson) Wentworth of Berwick, (or Shapleigh) Me., but I cannot verify Wentworth.

viii. Rebecca, m. Jonathan, s. of Josiah and Patience (Hanson) Clark of L.; pub. 15 Jan., 1820.
ix. Isaac, resided in Garland, Me.
x. Jacob, the youngest son, m. Narissa, daug. of Samuel Jones; resided in L.

FARNHAM.

24. David Farnham son of Matthew and Dorothy (Webber) Farnham of York, Me., was born in 1749; enlisted 5 May, 1775 in Capt. Eben'r Sullivan's Co. of Thirteenth Reg't. of Foot commanded by Col. James Scammon of the Army of the United Colonies of North America. He m. (1) at L. 26 Mch., 1779, Anna daug. of Samuel Wingate of Rochester, N. H., she d. 5 Mch., 1788, ae. 45 years, 6 mos. (g. s.) He m. (2) Mrs. Abigail (McDonald or Donald) Smith or Mrs. Abigail (Smith) Donald who d. 30 Sept., 1846, æ. 92 years, 3 mos. (g. s.)

Mr. Farnham resided in the westerly part of the town on the farm now (1896) known as the Mathew Farnham farm. He d. 6 Sept., 1814, ae. 65 years, (g. s.) and is buried in the "Camp Hill" Cemetery. Children by wife Anna:

i. Enoch, b. 17 June, 1779; bapt. 22 Oct., 1780.
ii. Samuel Wingate, b. 30, (month not given) 1781; bapt. 30 June, 1782; m. 5 Feb., 1808, Kate Wentworth; removed to Lewiston or Skowhegan, Me.
iii. Jeremiah, b. 21 July, 1784,; bapt. 28 July. 1786; resided in Somersworth, or Dover, N. H.
iv. Anna (or Nancy) b. 24 Feb., 1788; bapt. 20 Sept., 1789; m. John Libby of Lebanon.

Children by wife Abigail:

v. David, Jr., b. 23 March, 1790; bapt. 5 Sept., following: m. at Lebanon 29 Nov., 1810, Elizabeth, daug. of Jonathan and Elizabeth (Witherell) Burrows of Lebanon; he was drowned 21 April, 1824, ae. 34 years; she d. 28 Feb., 1840, æ. 51 years.
vi. John, b. 5 Feb., 1792; bapt. 31 July, 1793; resided in Lee, N. H.
vii. Joseph, } bapt. 4 July, 1795: killed by a falling frame, when young.
} Twins. b. 1 April, 1793.
viii. Benjamin, } bapt. 4 July, 1795; m. Susan Downs of Milton, } N. H.
ix. Mathew, b. 7 Aug., 1797; bapt. 29 Sept., 1797; resided in Mass. married, and returned to L.
x. Abigail, b. 12 Feb., 1798; bapt. 8 June, 1800; m. Thomas Wright of Dover, N. H.
xi. Dorothy, b. 6 Jan., 1802; bapt. 15 Aug., 1802; m. Ivory Gerrish of L.

25. Nathaniel Farnham of L. b. about 1752; described on the New Hampshire war rolls, as a "husbandman," "23" years of age; was in Capt. Jonathan Wentworth's Co. 13 June, 1775. This company was composed of men from Somersworth and Rochester, N. H., and from Berwick and Lebanon, Me. He was a private, living in Maine in 1820, as a pensioner. The Rev. Amos Main made the following entry in the Rochester First Church records: "1757, [April] 24 Baptized at Towow [Lebanon] Nath'l. Farnam."

He resided near the Moody Town Farm, but removed from town early, perhaps to Alfred, Me., where I find a Nathaniel Farnham resided in the last century.
He was of Lebanon when he m. at Berwick, Me., 1 March, 1779, Elizabeth Lord of Berwick.

26. RALPH[6] FARNHAM (Paul[5], Ralph[4], Ralph[3], Ralph[2], Ralph[1],) son of Paul and Elizabeth (Door) Farnham, became in 1778 one of the settlers of the West Parish, Shapleigh (now Acton) Me. His father Paul was a native of York, Me., where he was b. 20 Apr., 1730, but he d. at Acton, Me., in 1820. Paul Farnham was one of the original settlers of Lebanon where his son, the subject of this sketch. was born 20 June, 1756. The Rev. Amos Main of Rochester, N. H., bapt. him 5 Sept. following.
He enlisted 15 May, 1775, in Capt. Philip Hubbard's Co. of Col. James Scammon's Reg't. This regiment was stationed on Bunker Hill on the ever memorable 17 June, 1775.
A second time he enlisted as a private in Capt. Samuel Grant's Co. of Col. Oliver Titcomb's Reg't and received pay 18 July, 1777, for services for two months and for travelling *to* and *from* Rhode Island·
About 1778 he, his father Paul, his brothers Dummer, and Paul Jr. his uncle Ralph and his grandfather Philip Door removed from Lebanon to Shapleigh, Me. He resided on "Fox's Ridge" (now Acton) on the farm now (1896) owned and occupied by Charles Reynolds. In 1860 he visited Boston after Charles Sumner, in a speech delivered in Boston, had said that the last survivor of the Battle of Bunker Hill was dead : but the statement of Mr. Sumner was soon literally true. Ralph Farnham according to Mrs. Thomas Sherman's diary, died 9 Dec., 1860, ae. 104 years, 5 mo. 19 days. Children :

    i. BENJAMIN, who lived and died in Lebanon.
    ii. JOHN, m. widow Merrill and lived in Acton, Me.
    iii. DANIEL, who d. unmarried.
    iv. RALPH, JR.
    v. HANNAH, who m. Samuel Reynolds.
    vi. MARY, who m. Job Ricker.
    vii· JOANNA, who lived and died about 1875 in Boston, Mass., unmarried.

FOSS.

27. —— Foss, son of Benjamin Foss of Lebanon, was in the service in 1776 ; for, the Rev. Isaac Hasey recorded in his diary 14 Jan. 1776 . . . . "bill up by Benj. Foss for his *son* sick in ye Army." More I cannot state positively.

FROST.

28. MARK FROST, a native of Berwick, and a resident of Lebanon and Belgrade, Maine, was born about 1749 ; enlisted as a private April 1782 for three years, in Capt. John Williams's Co. of

Col. Joseph Vose's Reg't of the Mass. line; served two years, 7 mos., 26 days until 24 Dec., 1783; discharged at West Point by Gen. Henry Knox, commanding the American forces on the Hudson; applied for and received a pension 16 April, 1818; died at Belgrade, 5 Oct., 1835. His widow Hannah received the State bounty under the resolves of 1835-6.

In the Mass. Archives Vol. 34, p. 589 is the following: "Lebanon, May 27, 1782—Received of Mr. Ichabod Cowell, Chairman of Class No. 2 in Lebanon, £124 10s. in full for my bounty for engaging to serve three years as a Continental soldier for said Class. Witness: John Goodwin. (Signed) Mark frost." He m. at Berwick, Me., 25 Sept., 1770, Hannah Hersom.

He resided in Lebanon in the easterly part of the town on the farm now (1896) occupied by Frank Gerrish. He was a tithingman in the First Church, Lebanon, early in this century.

FURBISH. (FURBUSH.)

29. BENJAMIN FURBISH, Jr. was the son of Benjamin and Hannah Furbish who were the first of the name to settle in town, probably coming from Kittery, Me.

He enlisted 3 Sept, 1776, for 95 days in Capt. John Brewster's Co. of Col. Pierce Long's Reg't, stationed at New Castle, N. H. He was a private No. 54 of his Co. and received pay for extra services from 7 Dec., 1776, to 7 Jan'y, 1777.

He enlisted a second time as a private in Capt. Samuel Grant's Co. of Col. Oliver Titcomb's Reg't and received pay 18 July, 1777, for services for two months and for travelling *to* and *from* Rhode Island. On 18 May, 1777, Rev. Isaac Hasey recorded in his dairy: "Bill up by Furbish for himself *gone* into ye Army;" and again, 31 Aug., 1777, Mr. Hasey wrote:—"bill by Ben Furbish for his son *gone* in ye Army;" and again 5 Oct., he wrote: "Bill by Ben Furbish for his son in ye Army." On 7 Dec., 1777, Mr. Hasey recorded: "Bill of thanks by Ben furbish for his return from the Army." Often in his dairies Mr. Hasey called these men Furbish *Sr.* and Furbish *Jun*. On 28 March, 1776, he wrote: "Ben Furbish raised an House." The Rev. Isaac Hasey married on 7 Feb., 1781, Benjamin Furbish Junr. to Lydia Hussey at Robert Hussey's in Leb. (44). This man lived for some time on a lot situated in the westerly part of the town and about half way between the "Carr place," so called, and the farm now (1896) owned and occupied by Daniel Furbush. He removed from town eastward and none of his descendants are living in Leb. or vicinity, so far as I have opportunity to know.

GOODWIN.

30. JAMES GOODWIN was a private in a detachment of militia from the County of York under the command of Major Daniel Littlefield "on an expedition to Penobscott in compliance with a

resolve of the Honorable, the Council of this State [Mass.] passed June ye 29, 1779."

He enlisted 10 July; travelled 210 miles; served one month and twelve days; and was discharged 22 Aug., 1779.

He resided at West Lebanon on the farm now (1896) owned and occupied by Charles S. Orrell; but later removed to Berwick, Me., or Somersworth, N. H.

He married at Lebanon 1 Feb., 1781, Sarah, daughter of Tristam and Martha Copp of Lebanon. She was baptised 13 June, 1773, by Rev. Isaac Hasey.

31. JOHN GOODWIN was a captain of a company composed of Lebanon and Berwick men, "in a detachment of militia from the County of York under the command of Major Daniel Littlefield [of Wells] in an expedition to Penobscott in compliance with a resolve of the Honorable, the Council of this State [Mass.] passed June ye 29, 1779." He served from July 10, to Aug. 22, 1779.

He was a selectman in 1775 and 1776; and in 1782 he owned and occupied the original Ichabod Cowell farm which he exchanged in that year with Capt. William Chamberlain for his farm, the original David Twombly farm, near "Adams's Corner," in Rochester, N. H.

He removed to Rochester in Jany., 1783, and lived on that farm until about 1808 when he sold and moved away. He was called "Col." in 1782. He had sons John Jr., Joseph, and Benjamin. He had a sister Keziah who died unmarried.

On 18 April, 1776, "ye training band [of Lebanon] Chose John Goodwin for Capt." and on 19 May, 1778, Mr. Hasey wrote: "Capt. Goodwin draughting men." He seems to have been one of the most active men in the town during the Revolution according to Rev. Isaac Hasey's diary.

32. REUBEN GOODWIN, born about 1765, was a native of Berwick, Me., and a twin brother of Simeon (34).

He enlisted first in Capt. John Goodwin's Co. in "a detachment of militia from the County of York under the command of Major Daniel Littlefield on an expedition to Penobscott in compliance with a resolve of the Honorable, the Council of the State of Mass. passed June ye 29, 1779." He travelled 200 miles;was detached 10 July, 1779, and served two months. (See Mass. Archives, Vol. 37, p. 108).

He enlisted (Mass. Archives, Vol. 60, p. 74) at Berwick again as a private 10 April, 1782, for three years, and was in Capt. Abbott's Co. of Col. Tupper's Tenth Reg't., Mass. line, Continental Army; was transferred to Capt. Trotter's Co. of the Fifth Reg't; was again transferred to Capt. John Mills's Co. of Col. Joseph Vose's Reg't; continued in the service until the close of the war and remained about one year after the war to take care of the ordinances, artillery, and forts at West Point. He received two payments for services, one due 1 Jany., 1783, and another due 1 March, 1784. He also received a bounty from Berwick 24 May, 1782.

He stated these facts before Benjamin Greene, Chief Justice of the Circuit Court of Common Pleas for the First Eastern Circuit 19 Feb., 1819, in his affidavit made that day.

He removed to Lebanon about 1786, and was living here in 1836 at the age of 73 years, at which time he received a bounty from the State under the resolves of 1835-36.

He resided in the easterly part of the town, near the farm now (1896) owned and occupied by James M. Gerrish.

He m. at Berwick, Me., 6 Jan., 1785, Phebe Downs.

33. REUBEN GOODWIN, JR., b. about 1764, was a native of Berwick, Me. He enlisted as a private 26 April, 1781, for three years and joined the army at West Point in June, 1781. He was in Capt. Williams's Co. of the Fifth Mass. Reg't, General Patterson's Brigade. He continued in the service until Dec., 1783, when he was discharged, his discharge papers being signed by Gen'l Henry Knox. On the 1 March, 1784, he received three payments for services, due 1 Jan., 1782, 1 Jan., 1783, and 1 Jan., 1784. He was an inhabitant of Berwick when he enlisted, but soon after his term of service he removed to L. He received a bounty from Berwick (Mass. Archives, vol. 34, p. 559,) 9 May, 1781. He settled at North Lebanon the farm now (1896) owned and occupied by Newell Goodwin. He d. 14 Feb., 1827.

He m. at Berwick, Me., 10 Nov., 1785, Ruth Lord, who was b. about 1766, and who was living as his widow in L., a pensioner, 1 June, 1840 ; she also received a State bounty in 1836. The following imperfect record is submitted :—

  i. THOMAS, m. Betsey Glidden ; resided on homestead ; d. 9 May, 1856, æ. 59 years.
 ii. JACOB, m. Ruth. daug. of Rev. John and Abigail (Legro) Blaisdell of L.; resided at North Lebanon.
iii. JOEL, m. Elizabeth L., daug. of Isaac and Nancy (Libby) Hanscom of L.; she m. (2) Lyman Walker Lord of L.
Other children were : Reuben, Jr., Hannah, Polly, Olive, Betsey, Theodosia, Eunice, Ruth and Lucy.

34. SIMEON GOODWIN, a twin brother of Reuben (32) was born about 1765. He enlisted in Jan'y or March, 1783, for three years as a private in Capt. John Mills's Co. of Col. Joseph Vose's Reg't, Mass. line. He was transferred to Col. Hull's Reg't about six months before his discharge, which occurred in June, 1784, at West Point. His troops were among the last that were discharged.

He removed from Berwick to Lebanon in 1792, and resided in the easterly part of the town until his death, 21 April, 1836. His widow Mary, born about 1765, was living in Lebanon 1 June, 1840, having received a bounty from the State, and then receiving a pension from the government. From the town records the following children of Simeon and Mary Goodwin are arranged :

  i. LEMUEL, b. 24 Dec., 1787; died young, in Mass.
 ii. ASA, b. 24 Dec., 1789.
iii. HIRAM, b. 19 Jan., 1791; m. pub. 9 Aug., 1818, Draxey, daug. of Benjamin and Susan Gowell of L.

iv. Urban, b. 1 Jan., 1793; m. Pacia, daug. of Joshua Horne of L.
v. Dorothy, b. 16 Dec., 1795.
vi. Adan, born 28 April, 1797; m. Noah Pierce of L.
vii. Nancy, b. 2 Sept., 1800.
viii. Mark, b. 16 Feb., 1802: m. —— Wentworth.
ix. Horace, b. 6 Oct., 1806.
x. Luther, b. 6. Dec., 1808; m. Ruth. daug. of Simon Ricker of L.

Simeon Goodwin's wife was Mary Goodrich, whom he married at Berwick, 5 Nov., 1787.

GOWELL.

35. Benjamin Gowell, supposed native of Berwick, Me., was a private in Capt. Samuel Grant's Co. of Col. Storer's Reg't; enlisted 14 Aug. 1777; served three months and seven days in the Northern Army; discharged at Queman's Height, 4 Nov., 1777, when he was allowed fifteen days' traveling fee. He m. at Berwick, Me., 1 Sept. 1772, Susanna Pike.

After the Revolution he removed to the farm now (1896) known as the "Col. John Wentworth place," where he was living early in the present century. His widow Susan was residing with Wentworth Goodwin, Sr., her son-in-law, on 1 June, 1840, and a pensioner.

Children : Daughter Sally was published 6 Nov., 1819 to Wentworth Goodwin. She died in a few years and her sister Betsey was published 17 Dec., 1826, and married 11 Jan., 1827 to the same. Daughter Draxey was published 9 Aug., 1818 to Hiram s. of Simeon and Mary (Goodrich) Goodwin of Lebanon. Son Timothy lived and died in Rochester, N. H. Other sons were John, and another whose name is unknown is supposed to have removed to Belgrade, Me.

GRANT.

36. William Grant of Lebanon, son of William Grant Sr. was a Revolutionary pensioner. He was reputed to have had fifteen bullets shot through his coat and hat in a single battle from which he escaped uninjured. (Wentworth Genealogy).

On 23 Nov., 1769, he m, Mary, d. of Thomas and Mary (Nock) Wentworth who was born 11 Apr., 1742. They removed to Lebanon, where his wife died without issue 4 Sept., 1822. He adopted his nephew John Wentworth to whom he gave the homestead in Lebanon at his decease. (See Wentworth Genealogy).

HARTFORD.

37. Solomon Hartford was son of Stephen and Susannah (Wentworth) Hartford of Rochester, N. H. He removed to Leb. from which town he enlisted as a private in Capt. John Brewster's Co. of Col. Pierce Long's Reg't, stationed at New Castle, N. H. He was No. 60 of his Co. and served 95 days with extra pay from 7 Dec., 1776, to 7 Jany, 1777.

He m. 13 Sept., 1774 Mary or Mercy Farnham and resided in the

westerly part of the town on the Moses Ricker farm of 1870; later
he removed to Lancaster, N. H., where he lived on "Cherry
Mountain" until his death which occurred about 1832. He was
buried in Leb. on the Ricker farm, but his stone is unmarked.
Children:

    i. Elsie, b. Jan., 1776; m. 16 Feb., 1794, Nathaniel Tuttle of L.
    ii. Eliakim, b. 8 March, 1777: m. Charity, daug. of Richard and
        Abigail (Garland-Cook) Perkins of L. (64)
    iii. Sarah, b. 19 Nov., 1780; m. 19 Nov., 1799, Thomas Foss of L.
    iv. Susan, b. in 1783; m. Samuel Foss.
    v. Mercy, b. 1 Oct., 1786; m. Jeremiah Shorey of L.
    vi. William, b. Feb., 1789: m. Alphia Shorey, sister to Jeremiah.
    vii. Jennie, b. 18 April, 1792, m. Jonathan Ellis.
    viii. Meribah, b. Dec., 1794: m. Thomas Tibbetts.
    ix. Sobriety, b. June, 1797: m. Thomas Whitehouse.
    x. Solomon, Jr., b. 16 Jan., 1800: m. Ruth Tibbetts.
    xi. Machias, b. 30 March, 1803; m. Abigail Kilburn of Province-
        town. Mass.; lived in Boston.

HERSOM. (HORSOM.)

38. Benjamin Hersom (Horsom), a native of Berwick, Me.,
enlisted from that town, as corporal, in Capt. Samuel Grant's Co. of
Col. Storer's Reg't 14 Aug., 1777. He served with the Northern
army two months and twenty-five days and was discharged at Queman's Height 23 Oct., 1777.

He removed from Berwick to Lebanon where he was the first
settler on the farm now (1896) owned and occupied by Fred Hersom at North Lebanon. He married at Berwick, Me., 13 April,
1780, Dorcas Ricker, and died about 1836 aged not far from 80
years. Children:

    i. Jonathan, m. 2 July, 1812, Eunice Nock (Knox) of L. (53.)
    ii. Abigail. m. William Hurd of Acton, Me.
    iii. Dorcas, m. Josiah Witham of Acton. Me.
    iv. Sally, m. —— Sanborn of Somersworth. N. H.
    v. Betsey, m. Love Roberts of Lebanon. (73.)
    vi. Esther. m. Samuel Pray of Lebanon.

39. David Hersom, a native of Berwick, Me., was born 18 May,
1760. He enlisted in Capt. Stephen Hodsdon's Co. of the Mass.
militia for two months in the spring of 1775; marched to Kittery
Point and served there and at Portsmouth Harbor. James Goodwin
was lieutenant of the company, or ensign; and this one company
only was sent to defend the town from the British ship "Scar-
borough" then lying in the Harbor.

He again enlisted in March 1776 in Capt. Place's Co., Thomas
Hodsdon, lieutenant; Aaron Hanson, ensign; marched to Mystic
and Cambridge, thence to New York and Canada, in Col. James
Reed's Reg't; served for one year.

At the special request of Gen. John Sullivan while at Trenton, he
remained six weeks after his term expired during which time he was
one of the advanced guard in the battle of Princeton.

In the latter part of the summer of 1777, he enlisted for a third
time, in Capt. Samuel Grant's Co. of Mass. militia for three months;

marched to Saratoga, and assisted in the capture of Gen Burgoyne's army. His regiment was commanded by Col. Joseph Storer.

In the spring or summer of 1778 his fourth enlistment occurred, in Capt. Sadwell's Co. of Col. Joseph Cilley's Reg't., New Hampshire line; he marched to New Jersey and Pennsylvania where he served for nine months.

In the autumn of 1779 he enlisted at Portsmouth, N. H., on board the "Ranger" for one year. The ship soon took a prize which was retaken by the British in about three weeks; and Hersom, with 600 or 700 others, was carried a prisoner to the West Indies where he was confined for six months.

He was taken by a British fleet to Charleston, S. C., where he was detained for some time, reaching home after about one year. He was a pensioner under Act of Congress 18 March, 1818, and by Act of 7 June, 1832, received $84 per year.

He stated in his affidavit, No. 793, in Land Office, Augusta, Me., that he was at one time an inhabitant of Lebanon. This man, or another of same name, m. at Berwick in 1808 Lydia Nock.

40. JACOB HERSOM, (Hossom) supposed native of Berwick, Me., enlisted as a private 3 Sept., 1776, in Capt. John Brewster's Co. of Col. Pierce Long's Reg't, stationed at New Castle, N. H. He was No. 48 of his Co.; served 95 days and was paid for extra service from 7 Dec., 1776, to 7 Jan., 1777. He was a pensioner living in 1820. He is probably *the* Jacob Hersom who m. Lydia daug. of Philip and Lydia (Mason) Door of Leb. and after 1770 of Shapleigh, Me. He lived in, or not far from, the town of Leb.

41. JONATHAN HERSOM (Horsom) probably a native of Berwick, Me., served in the Revolution twice. He was in Capt. Place's Co. of Col. James Reed's Reg't. He marched to Cambridge, thence to New York and to Canada in 1776. In this Co. Thomas Hodsdon was Lieut. and Aaron Hanson, Ensign.

On 31 Aug., 1777, Mr. Hasey's dairy states:—"bill by Mrs. Jona". Horsom for her husband gone in ye Army." In Mass. Archives, Vol. 22, p. 198, he is described as a private in Capt. Elisha Shapleigh's Co. of Col. Joseph Storer's Reg't enlisting 14 Aug., 1777, and being discharged 23 Oct. following, after serving 2 mos., 25 days. The pay roll was dated at Kittery, Me., and included 15 days travel.

He became a resident of Leb. living in the northeasterly part of the town on the road leading from "Hanscom's Corner" to Acton and about one mile from said "Corner." By an affidavit in the Land Office at Augusta it seems that he was living in 1836 at the age of 74 years. He m. at Berwick, Me., 18 Dec., 1780, Martha Goodrich.

42. SAMUEL HERSOM (Horsom) of Lebanon, born about 1763, was a private in Capt. *Esaias* Preble's Co. of Col. Jacob Gerrish's Reg't. He enlisted 2 April and was discharged 3 July, 1778, serving three mouths and five days. Gerrish's regiment of guards was

stationed at Winter Hill, Charlestown (now Somerville). Mr. Hersom was a Revolutionary pensioner residing with Nathaniel Hersom,
in Lebanon, 1 June, 1840, at the age of 77 years.

He resided on the "Middle Cross-Road" so called, about two
miles southeast of the center of the town. He d. at Lebanon 24
Dec., 1843. He had a brother Joshua, and also sons, Oliver,
Daniel, and Samuel Jr. Oliver m. at L. 17 March, 1816, Phebe
Ricker.

He m. at Berwick, Me., 3 June, 1784, Arnia Goodrich.

HILL.

43. Jeremiah Hill, b. 15 May, 1767, who was in the employ of
Col. Carr of Somersworth, N. H., during the Revolution, was for a
time in the army—perhaps in the regular army between 1783 and
1787. On 3 Oct., 1787, he married at Lebanon Abigail daug. of
Samuel and Abigail Stevens of L. She was b. 22 June, 1760. For
some years he resided near the farm now (1896) owned by the heirs
of Dea. Joseph Fernald, but removed to Alfred Gore, Me., where
he continued his occupation as miller. His children were :

    i. Eleanor, b. 22 May, 1788; bapt. 10 Sept., 1798; m. Benjamin
        Farnham.
    ii. Jeremiah, Jr., b. July, 1790; bapt. 10 Sept., 1798; was in Second
        War with Great Britian.
    iii. Daniel, b. 7 March, 1798; bapt. 10 Sept., 1798; resided in Mil-
        ton, N. H.
    iv. Sally, bapt. 10 Sept., 1798.
    v. Lydia Grove, b. 15 April, *1802; bapt. 23 June, *1799; m. Moses
        Downs of Milton, N. H.
    vi. Lovey, bapt. 2 Aug., 1801; died unmarried.

HUSSEY.

44. Robert Hussey of Lebanon enlisted as a private 24 Sept.,
1776, in Capt. Abraham Perkins's Co. of Col. Pierce Long's Reg't.,
stationed at New Castle, N. H.

He was No. 42 and remained with his company and regiment until 7 Jan'y., 1777, when he received advanced pay for one month ;
but when ordered to march to Ticonderoga on 13 Jan'y he refused,
claiming that he was subject to the military orders of Mass. and not
those of New Hampshire whose authorities issued the orders. He
lived upon the farm in the southerly part of the town, now (1896)
owned and occupied by Albert J. Betts. He removed from town in
1787. The First Parish records contain the following facts relating
to the family of Robert and Lydia Hussey :

    i. Sarah, bapt. 27 June, 1773.
    ii. John, bapt. 1 June, 1777.
    iii. Lydia, bapt. 4 July, 1779; m. 7 Feb., 1781, Benjamin Furbish,
        Jr. (29)
    iv. Reuben, bapt. 11 Nov., 1781.

The records also show that Benjamin Hussey married 17 March,

---

*The town and parish records show this inconsistency.

1774, Sarah Harmon, and that their daughter Mercy was baptized 18 June, 1775, and Betsey 1 Dec., 1776. No further mention is made in the records of either family.

JAMES.

45. ELISHA JAMES, son of John who was first of the name to settle in Lebanon, was born about 1755.

He enlisted 5 May, 1775, in Capt. Philip Hubbard's Co. of Col. James Scammon's Reg't. Capt. Hubbard was of Berwick and subsequently of Shapleigh, Me. Col. Scammon was of Pepperellborough (now Saco), and his regiment was on Bunker Hill 17 June following; but on account of some misunderstanding his regiment was not engaged in the battle of that day. Mr. James returned 2 July, 1775.

He m. 12 Oct., 1774, at Lebanon Mercy Tebbetts, and removed 29 Dec., 1777, to Shapleigh (now Acton) Me. He first resided in Lebanon on a lot known as the "James lot," situated about half way between the "Camp Hill" Cemetery and the residence of Noah B. Lord. In Shapleigh he resided near Hubbard's Corner, but moved back to Lebanon about 1810. He purchased a lot some two miles from any highway; and in fourteen days after going on to it with carpenters, he had a well constructed house which has served the town in recent years in sheltering the poor. This place is now (1896) known as the "Bog Town Farm."

He d. in L. in 1825, ae. 70; his widow Mercy d. in 1826, ae. 69. Issue were:

    i. SALLY. m. 1797, John, son of John and Miriam (White) Bodwell of Shapleigh, (now Acton) Me.; she d. 1846; he b. 5 Oct., 1776; d. in 1860.
    ii. JOHN, enlisted in the War of 1812; went to New York where he died in Camp.
    iii. SAMUEL. m. —— Pugsley of Sanford, Me.; removed to Ohio.
    iv. ELISHA, JR., d. at the age of 15 years.
    v. DANIEL, m. Dorothy, daug. of Rev. John and Abigail (Legro) Blaisdell of L.; resided on the James homestead in the "Bog"; was a charter member of Second Free Baptist Church of L. in 1834.
    vi. OLIVE, m. Jethro Hurd; resided in Acton and later in Sanford, Me.
    vii. PATIENCE, m. John Drew of Shapleigh, (now Acton) Me.
    viii. MEHITABLE, m. Thaddeus Ricker of L.

46. JOHN JAMES, supposed brother of Elisha, son of John, who was first of the name to settle in town. He enlisted 5 May, 1775, in Capt. Eben'r Sullivan's Co. of the Thirteenth Reg't of Foot, commanded by Col. James Scammon, and belonging to the Army of the United Colonies of North America.

Again he appears as a private from Lebanon in Capt. John Goodwin's Co. "in a detachment of Militia from the County of York, under command of Major Daniel Littlefield on an expedition to Penobscott in compliance with a resolve of the Honorable, the Council of this

State [Mass.] passed June y⁶ 29, 1779." He served two months, from 10 July to 10 Sept., 1779, and travelled 210 miles.

He married at Lebanon 26 March, 1779, Lydia Door, and he, or another of the same name, was receiving a pension in 1820, and residing in Maine, when he was enumerated as a private of the Mass. line, Revolutionary War.

KENNERSON.

47. JOHN KENNERSON, JR., of Lebanon, born about 1763, son of John Kenerson, was a private, enlisting at Berwick, Me., 20 Dec., 1781; mustered by Col. Ichabod Goodwin of Berwick, but in 1818 known as Gen. Ichabod Goodwin. He went to Boston where he was ordered to join the army at West Point. He was attached to Lieut. Seldin's Co. of the Fourth Mass. Reg't; was waiter to General McDougal for one year; then joined his company, and continued with it until the close of the war; discharged at or near West Point, 31 Dec., 1783, having served two years and eleven days.

He married at Lebanon 1 April, 1784, Betsey Fall, the Rev. Isaac Hasey performing the marriage. She was born about 1757, and was living in 1834 at the age of 87 years.

He moved from Lebanon to Denmark, Maine, about 1794, where he died 29 Oct., 1833. He was a pensioner from 1818 until his death. They had a son, David B., born in 1785, and living in Denmark, Me., in 1844. His widow, Betsey, received a bounty from the State in 1844. The surname, in affidavit No. 834, Land Office, Augusta, is spelled *Kenerson, Kenison, Kinerson, Kennerson, Keniston* and *Kennison*. Widow Betsey states in her affidavit that she never could read nor write a *word*, which may partially account for the propagation of confusion in the nomenclature of this subject.

A John Keneson received in Aug. 1777, a bounty of Capt. Enoch Page, in command of New Hampshire troops, to march to Rhode Island and Conn.

48. JOSEPH KENNISON of Lebanon, born in 1745, enlisted from Lebanon 13 June, 1775, as a private, in Capt. Jonathan Wentworth's Co; called "husbandman, aged 30."

He enlisted again in Capt. Daniel Gordon's Co. 13 July, 1780; discharged 25 Oct. following. His company was in Col. Thomas Bartlett's New Hampshire Reg't raised for the defence of West Point.

He resided in Lebanon from 1773 to 1787 when he removed from town. His farm was on the east side of the "Great Brook," so called, near the P. & R. R. R. He set a fire 25 August, 1774, which destroyed hay and fence belonging to the Rev. Isaac Hasey whose lot joined his on the west. He married at Lebanon 6 Oct., 1773, Sarah Bean, the ceremony being performed by "Parson" Hasey.

49. SAMUEL KENNISON of Lebanon was mustered into the service between 30 May and 13 June, 1777 by Joseph Bragdon of York.

He served in Capt. Samuel Derby's Co. of Col. John Bailey's Battalion. (See Mass. Archives, Vol. 43, p. 94).

KNOX. (NOCK.)

50. DAVID[5] KNOX (Nock), (Zachariah[4], Zachariah[3], Sylvanus[2], Thomas[1]), was a son of Zachariah and Judith (Pitman) Nock of Berwick, Me. His name occurs in a list of men raised for the six months' service and returned by Brig. Gen. Paterson under date at Camp Totoway 25 Oct., 1780. On a descriptive list in Mass. Archives he appears as "17 years of age, five feet six inches in stature, of ruddy complexion, residence Berwick; arrived at Springfield, Mass., 1 Aug. 1780, in the 32d Division under command of Lieut. Benjamin Pike." On 18 Dec., 1781, the selectmen ef Berwick paid him a bounty for three years' service.

In 1820 he was a Revolutionary pensioner then living in Lebanon. There is a tradition that he was a waiter on Major André, the British spy, during André's confinement and execution in Sept., 1780. He was discharged 1 Feb., 1781, having served at West Point. On 6 Sept, 1792, he married at L. Molly Hanson, probably the daughter of Daniel Hanson of L., who was bapt. by the Rev. Isaac Hasey, 19 July, 1773.

He resided at L. on the farm now (1896) owned and occupied by William Furbush Wentworth at "Poplar Hill" so called.
Children :

    i. PATIENCE, b. 27 Feb., 1793; m. Joshua Knox of Berwick, Me.
    ii. ENOCH, b. 12 Aug., 1795; d. 15 Nov., 1795.
    iii. DAVID, JR., b. 4 Oct., 1796; m. Hannah Cook of Topsham, Me.; drowned while driving logs.
    iv. LEVI, b. 7 May, 1799; d. 15 Nov., 1857.
    v. JERUSHA, b. 3 May, 1801; m. Amos Pray of Shapleigh, Me.; d. 1 July, 1862.
    vi. MARY, b. 3 June, 1803; twice married.
    vii. LYDIA, b. 5 June, 1805; m. Edmund Short of Newburyport, Mass.
    viii. BARZILLA, b. 27 Feb., 1807; m. Martha Hanson, of Berwick, Me.
    ix. LEONARD, b. 18 April, 1810; m. Mrs. Hannah (Cook) Knox; resided in Biddeford, Me.
    x. HANSON, b. 30 Sept., 1812; d. 3 Dec., 1815.
    xi. MERCY HANSON, b. 6 Dec., 1815; m. Moses Cooper of Dover, N. H.

51. ELEAZER KNOX (Nock), of Lebanon, born in 1754, is described in Mass. Archives, Vol. 35, p. 221, as "26 years of age; five feet, eight inches in stature; of dark complexion; marched 1 June, 1780, arrived at Springfield, Mass., 31 Aug., 1780; assigned to the Thirty-ninth Division of six months' men; marched from Springfield under the care of Ensign Simonds 7 Sept., 1780; discharged 1 Dec., 1780."

In 1784, he received a bounty from Lebanon for his services of six months in the Revolution.

On 19 March, 1779, the Rev. Isaac Hasey joined in wedlock Eleazer Nock and Marcy Spencer.

52. JOHN[5] KNOX (Nock), (Zachariah[4], Zachariah[3], Sylvanus[2], Thomas[1]) was the eldest son of Zachariah and Judith (Pitman) Nock of Berwick, Me.

He enlisted from Berwick between 30 May and 13 June, 1777, in Capt. Samuel Darby's (Derby's) Co. of Col. John Bailey's Battalion. He was mustered by Joseph Bragdon of York who wrote his surname "*Noox*" on the muster-roll now in Mass. Archives. He was a private and was in the service at Valley Forge 25 Jan., 1778. He served from 1 May, 1777, to 31 Dec., 1779, and from 1 Jan., 1780 to 21 May following, having enlisted for three years.

He married Molly Grant and removed to Lebanon where he settled on a lot situated on the east side of the road leading from "Legro's Corner" to "Poplar Hill," which lot now (1896) forms a part of the pasture owned by Noah Emery Lord. He was a pensioner living in town in 1820. Children :

    i. SAMUEL, m. 29 Nov., 1792, Sally Gerrish.
    ii, JOHN, JR., m. 16 April, 1795, Sarah, daug. of Henry and Frances (Stevens) Door of Lebanon; was old-time singing master.
    iii. EUNICE, m. 12 Dec., 1788, Thomas, s. of John and Sarah Legro of L., as his second wife; she d. 23 Dec., 1823, æ. 53 years. (g. s.)
    iv. MOLLY, m. Parker Hodsdon of L.
    v. EDWARD, m. 23 March, 1810, Sarah Burrows of L.
    vi. WILLIAM, farmer, m. 26 Dec., 1805, his cousin Betsey, daug. of Jonathan and Betsey (Knox) Knox of Berwick, Me.; she was b. 6 March, 1785, and married second Jeremiah Lord of L. He resided on the old homestead in L. and was a soldier in the War of 1812.
    vii. LUCETTA, m. Fisher Pinkham of Milton, N. H.

53. ZACHARIAH[5] KNOX (Nock), (Zachariah[4], Zachariah[3], Sylvanus[2], Thomas[1]) was the third child of Zachariah and Judith (Pitman) Nock of Berwick, Me.

He was a private in Capt. Ebenezer Sullivan's Co. of Col. James Scammon's Maine Reg't and enlisted 5 May, 1775, serving three months and three days. On another roll he is described as "of Berwick, 25 years of age, five feet five inches in stature, of light complexion," belonging to Capt. Hamilton's Second Reg't, raised by the resolve of 20 Apr., 1778.

He resided in Lebanon near the center of the town on the farm now (1896) owned and occupied by the heirs of David Hersom. His wife was Martha Naylor, and he d. in 1816. Children :

    i. BENJAMIN, d. in Lebanon.
    ii. DAVID, was killed at Ossipee, N. H.
    iii. EUNICE, m. 2 July, 1812, at L., Jonathan, s. of Benjamin and Dorcas (Ricker) Hersom of L. (38)

LIBBY.

53½. SAMUEL LIBBY served in the Revolutionary army according to reliable statements, but I have been unable to find exact statements of his military service. He was the son of Daniel Libby of Berwick, Me., where he was born 24 Aug., 1760. He m. Betsey Hardison 3 Jan., 1782, and d. about 1827 ; she d. 1834. He was a tanner and farmer having settled on or near the farm in the easterly part of the town, now (1896) owned by Abraham Hanscom. Children :

i. POLLY, m. 29 Dec., 1811, Hiram Pray, as second wife.
ii. NANCY, m. Isaac Hanscom of L.
iii. THOMAS, died of disease contracted in War of 1812.
iv. PARMELIA, m. 1809, Hiram Pray, as first wife.
v. ELIZA, d. young, at Nathan Cogswell's in Berwick.
vi. NAHUM, m. Dolly ——; was sadler at Topsham, Me.; d. in 1823.
vii. SALLY, b. 28 March, 1795; m. 28 Nov., 1816, Paul Wentworth.
viii. JOHN, m. Polly Hodgdon.
ix. BETSEY, m. —— Lancaster.
x. WILLIAM PEPPERELL, b. 12 Dec., 1803; m. Sarah Drown.
xi. CHARLOTTE, m. Hiram Pray.

LORD.

54. ELISHA LORD, baptized at Berwick, Me., 28 April, 1765, was son of Elisha and Sarah Lord of Berwick, where he was born about 1761. Elisha Lord, the father, was son of Capt. Abraham and Margaret (Gowen) Lord. Capt. Abraham was son of Nathan Lord, Jr., and grandson of Nathan Lord, Sr., the emigrant from Stackpole Court, Pembrokeshire, Wales, to the ancient settlement at Kittery, Maine.

Elisha Lord, the soldier, was twice in the Revolutionary army. He enlisted 14 Aug., 1777, in Capt. Samuel Grant's Co. of Col. Joseph Storer's Reg't; served with the Northern army two months and twenty-five days and was discharged at Queman's Height, 23 Oct., 1777.

In Vol. 74. p. 171 of Mass. Archives, he is described as enlisting 24 Nov., 1781, for three years in Capt. Joseph Bates's Co. of Lt. Col. J. Brooks's 7th Reg't. The roll dated at "York Hutts" 6 Feb., 1782, shows him to have been "20 years of age, 5 feet 6 in. in stature, of light complexion, with brown hair." He was a laborer, enlisted as a private and received a bounty from Berwick, 18 Dec., 1781. He was a pensioner, under the Act of Congress of 18 March, 1818, and was living in Lebanon in 1820.

On 27 June, 1787 he married at Berwick, Dorcas Goodwin. He, with other members of the family, removed to Lebanon where he is supposed to have received a grant of land for his military services. The lot upon which he first lived is now (1896) owned by Noah B. Lord and is situated on the northwesterly side of his farm; later he removed to the farm of the late Thomas Millet Wentworth, Esq., where on Sunday, 8 June, 1806, his wife and the wife of Daniel Roberts were both killed by lightning in the Wentworth house upon returning from church.

In his last years he lived with David Farnham, Jr., who cared for him until his death. His grave is in the northeasterly corner of the Farnham field, unmarked. Children :

i. EUNICE, b. 26 Feb., 1788; m. Joseph Wentworth.
ii. JOHN, m. Susan Palmer.
iii. IVORY, d. when about 15 years of age.

iv. BENJAMIN, b. 1795; m. Keziah, daug. of Noah and Keziah (Brackett) Lord of L. He d. 13 June, 1856, æ. 61 years.
v. DORCAS, d. unmarried.
vi, ELIZA, d. unmarried.

55. NATHAN LORD, Sr., son of Ebenezer and Martha (Emery) Lord of Berwick, Maine, was born 26 Jany., 1757 (g. s.)

He was a private 5 Nov., 1775, at Kittery Point under Capt. Stephen Hodgdon; enlisted as a private 16 Sept., 1776, in Capt. William McDuffee's Co., mustered by Stephen Evans in the Second New Hampshire Reg't "to join the Continental army in New York."

He, the Lebanon Nathan Lord, enlisted as a private for three years 19 May, 1777, and served in Capt. Pillsbury's, Smith's, and Capt. Samuel Derby's Co.'s, of Col. John Bailey's Battalion, of Cols. Wiggleworth's, Sprout's and Smith's Reg'ts, Mass. line. He served until 19 May, 1780, when he was discharged at West Point. He was a pensioner from 16 March, 1819. (Land Office Files, Augusta.)

There were living in Berwick about 1776, two Nathan Lords, and while I know that the last paragraph relates to the Lebanon Nathan, I am not positive that the paragraph preceding relates to him.

He married first 26 March, 1781, Mercy (Knox) Downs, a widow, who was born 21 Jany, 1755; she died at Lebanon 22 Nov., 1810 (g. s.)

He married second 25 Nov., 1811, at Rochester, N. H., Sarah Wingate, daughter of Benjamin(?) Wingate of Rochester; she was living in 1835. He died at Lebanon, 26 Nov., 1833 ae. 76 years, 10 mos., and is buried on the farm then owned by him; but now (1896) owned and occupied by John R. Chamberlain at Lebanon Center.

He was a politician of note, of the Jeffersonian party. He was on the Committee appointed in 1800 to lay out the First Parish Cemetery.

His children by wife Mercy were:

    i. BENJAMIN, b. 28 April, 1788: d. 6 Oct., 1863; he m. Mercy Fall, born about 1791; she d. 6 Feb., 1867, æ. 76 years, 2 months; resided in Lebanon. Mercy was sister to Nathan's wife.
    ii. NATHAN, JR., was a selectman in 1821, '22. '23, '24; removed to Somersworth, N. H. He m. Abra, daug. of George and —— (Kennerson) Fall of L.

56. SIMEON LORD, son of Ebenezer and Martha (Emery) Lord of Berwick, Me., was born in Dec., 1750.

He enlisted from Berwick 8 May, 1775, in Capt. Philip Hubbard's Co. of Col. James Scammon's Reg't, composed of men from the District of Maine. He was a sergeant in his company and in all probability was at Bunker Hill on 17 June following.

He occupied a farm in Lebanon about one and one-half miles southeast of the Center, which farm is now (1896) owned and occupied by James Lord. He married Mary Hersom, but died without issue. Tradition relates that while in the Revolution, he was in a scouting party which was surprised and surrounded by a large force of British. Sergeant Lord immediately ordered his men to fire a volley. His brother Nathan, who was a private, dashed out in front of the ranks and said, "A running fire or they will kill us all." The command of the private, who took in the situation at a glance, was obeyed. He m. at Berwick, Me., 15 Aug., 1774, Mary Hersom.

LEGRO.

57. DAVID LEGRO, son of John and Sarah Legro, who were settlers in Lebanon as early as 1771, was born in 1759; and removed with his parents to Lebanon.

He enlisted as a private in Capt. Jedediah Goodwin's Co. of Col. Edward Wigglesworth's Reg't. Jedediah Goodwin, captain, was of Berwick, and Ichabod Cowell, lieutenant, was of Lebanon. The company set out for Canada, and Legro was discharged at Albany 30 Nov., 1776.

He then re-enlisted as a private in Capt. Samuel Grant's Co. of Col. Oliver Titcomb's Reg't, and received pay, 18 July, 1777, for services for two months, and for travelling to and from Rhode Island. Capt. Grant was of Berwick.

He returned to Lebanon, and 19 Jan., 1785, was "joined in wedlock" to Betsey, daughter of Capt. John and Hannah (Waldron) Hayes of Dover, N. H., and of Lebanon.

He engaged in the manufacture of potash, adding later a grocery store and tavern at "Legro's Corner," as the hamlet was then called.

He was the fifth person to be chosen to represent Lebanon at the General Court of Mass., and he continued a representative from 1805 to 1813 inclusive, also from 1815 to 1817 inclusive. In 1809 he was a selectman. When the Constitutional Convention was called at Portland in 1819, he and Daniel Wood were chosen as the delegates from Lebanon. Daniel Wood acted with the minority; David Legro with the majority in that convention, hence David Legro became one of the signers of the Constitution of Maine. Daniel Wood being one of the thirty-one members who objected to that Constitution, claimed as the chief objection that it provided for an unjust apportionment of representatives.

Mr. Legro became the *first* representative from Lebanon to the new State of Maine in 1820 and 1821. He was a justice of the peace from 1821 to 1829, by which he acquired the title of "Squire." He was a freemason and accumulated a good property. He died at Lebanon 21 Aug., 1835, without children, æ. 76 years. His widow died 27 Sept., 1839, æ. 73 years. (g. s.)

His brother Thomas enlisted in the army in the Spring of 1780 for three years, but as he was needed at home a substitute was procured and he did not enter the service. (Land Office files, Augusta.)

58. JOHN LEGRO, son of John and Sarah Legro who settled in Lebanon as early as 1771, was mustered 25 Nov., 1775, by Capt. George Turner into Capt. David Copp's Co., which company of "Minutemen" was raised pursuant to an order of the Committee of Safety issued 12 Oct., 1775. A portion of this company went to

Winter Hill, Charlestown (now Somerville) to take the place of the retiring Conn. troops. He was No. 11 of his company.

On 22 March, 1779, he was married at Lebanon to Patience Blaisdell. He resided for a time on the farm now (1896) owned and occupied by Frank Lord; but removed to Bangor, Maine, before 1812.

MARTIN. (MARDIN.)

59. THOMAS MARTIN (or Mardin) (colored) was a Revolutionary pensioner who resided in Lebanon many years. It is certain that he received a pension and it is claimed that he enlisted from New Jersey. He left no descendants and is one of the few colored persons that ever resided in town. He died in Leb. unmarried.

McCRILLIS.

60. ROBERT McCRILLIS was the son of Daniel and Elizabeth (Thompson) McCrillis of Lebanon. His father, Daniel McCrillis, the original McCrillis to settle in town, is said to have been a Scotch-Irish emigrant who came to Leb. from the north of Ireland soon after 1745.

This family was probably living in Lebanon before 1750, for on 30 July, 1749, the Rev. Amos Main entered upon the records of the First Parish of Rochester, N. H., the following: "Also Baptized Robert McCrelis." At that time the Rochester church was located about four miles from where the McCrillises lived in L.

Robert McCrillis was a private in Capt. David Place's Co., stationed on Seavey's Island, being named on a return dated 5 Nov., 1775.

On 14 July, 1776, the Rev. Isaac Hasey of the First Parish of Lebanon recorded in his diary as follows:

"Bill up by Rob't McCrellis for himself bound into ye Army." His name occurs on a roll dated at Charlestown 27 July, 1776, in Capt. John Drew's Co. raised for Canada out of Col. Evans's and Col. Badger's Reg'ts. See Canney. (5)

MERROW.

61. JOSHUA MERROW, born in 1753, is described as of "Rochester," N. H., "aged 22 years," "husbandman," in Capt. Jonathan Wentworth's Co. enlisting 13 June, 1775.

He was an ensign commissioned 2 April, 1777, in the Second New Hampshire Reg't. He was at White Plains 29 Aug., 1778. In a petition addressed to the Legislature of N. H., in 1778, he states that he lost his baggage and clothing at Ticonderoga, where he was captured and carried a captive into Canada; that after great suffering and hardships he was transported to New York; and then returned to his regiment in New Hampshire in 1778.

He was commissioned a lieutenant 12 July, 1780, and remained in the army until 28 Feb., 1783, or later.

He was probably a son of Samuel and Abigail Merrow of Rochester, N. H., where he married Peggy Garland of Rochester, 28 Oct., 1788, the Rev. Joseph Haven performing the marriage.

A Joshua Merrow, supposed to be the same person, was living on a lot that now (1896) is owned by the heirs of Charles B. Chamberlain. He sold this lot to Ralph Blaisdell in 1780, when he removed from town. His name is perpetuated in "Merrow's Bridge," and "Merrow's Corner," near where his house once stood.

MILLS.

62. JOHN MILLS, Sr. is described in the Mass. Archives, Vol. 19, p. 161, as "of Lebanon," "a private" in Capt. Jedediah Goodwin's Co. of Col. Edward Wigglesworth's Reg't. On 22 July, 1776, the company set out for Canada, and Mills was discharged at Albany, N. Y., 30 Nov. following.

He enlisted again in 1777 in Patterson's Co. of Baldwin's Reg't of the Mass. line and served under Gen. Henry Knox. Several years before his death which occurred 21 Dec., 1810, he removed from L. to Belgrade, Me., where his widow Mary was living at the age of 80 years and upwards in July, 1835. On 25 Aug., 1837, she received a bounty from the State provided under the resolves of 1835-6. The Rev. Mr. Hasey entered in his diary, 6 Oct., 1776 : "Bill up by Molly Mills for her husband in ye army," etc. He had a son, as I conjecture, of the same name, for Hasey wrote : 1 April, 1784, John Mills Jun'. and Peggy Kenison were married."

PERKINS.

63. EPHRAIM PERKINS of Lebanon was mustered between 10 March, and 17 March, 1777, by Joseph Bragdon of York.

He belonged to Capt. Samuel Derby's Co. of Col. John Bailey's Batt°. (Mass. Archives, Vol. 43, p. 139.)

An Ephraim Perkins died at Rochester, N. H., 31 Jany., 1823, aged 80 years and his widow died 18 Oct., 1823, aged 90 years, but I am not sure that both name the same person.

64. GILBERT PERKINS, one of the early settlers of Lebanon, first enlisted 20 July, 1775, in Capt. Philip Hubbard's Co. of Col. James Scammon's Reg't.

He re-enlisted from Lebanon, 3 Sept., 1776, as a private in Capt. John Brewster's Co. of Col. Pierce Long's Reg't, stationed at New Castle, N. H. ; and was mustered and paid by Otis Baker. He remained in Long's Reg't until 7 Jan., 1777.

He was married at Rochester, N. H., 20 Aug., 1749, to Charity, daug. of Stephen and Susannah (Wentworth) Hartford ; and was the first settler on the farm in the westerly part of Lebanon now (1896) owned and occupied by the heirs of Lewis Ricker. He removed from town eastward. He had a son Richard (65).

65. RICHARD PERKINS enlisted 5 May, 1775, in Capt. Philip Hubbard's Co. of Col. James Scammon's Reg't. Scammon's regi-

ment of Maine men was at Bunker Hill on 17 June following, but
on account of a misunderstanding of orders was not in the battle on
that day.

Perkins was a Revolutionary pensioner late in his life. He married at Lebanon, 13, or 18 May, or June, 1779, Mrs. Abigail (Garland) Cook, widow of David Cook (11) of Lebanon and daug. of
Dodivah Garland of Leb. He resided for a time on the farm now
(1896) owned and occupied by the heirs of Lewis Ricker, but removed to Rochester, N. H., 11 March, 1783, and later to Jefferson,
N. H., where he died about 1832. He was the son of Gilbert and
Charity (Hartford) Perkins, early settlers of Leb. (64).

PIERCE.

66. JOSEPH PIERCE, born in 1754, is described in Mass. Archives,
Vol. 29, p. 57, as "of Lebanon, County of York; 25 years of age;
five feet, eight inches in stature : of light complexion; delivered to
Lieut. Lilley, 1779."

PINNER. (PENNEY?)

67. JOHN PINNER, (Penney?) born in 1760, is described in
Mass. Archives, Vol. 45, p. 282, as "19 years of age; five feet,
three inches in stature; light complexion; engaged in the Fourth
Co. of the Second Reg't to reinforce the Continental Army for nine
months, agreeable to a resolve of the General Court of the State of
Mass. Bay, passed 9 June, 1779.

He is further described in Vol. 29, p. 116, as "belonging to Lebanon; enlisted Nov., 1779, in Capt. Allen's Co. in the First Mass.
Regiment. He enlisted for three years or during the war and served
until 1 Jan., 1781.

I have no evidence excepting the above, that anyone bearing the
surname Pinner ever resided in Lebanon; and I conjecture that the
above named person either enlisted under an assumed name, or resided in Lebanon for a short time only; or that the name Pinner
should have been written Penney. I have found many errors in the
spelling of names on the war rolls.

PRICE. (PIERCE?)

68. STEPHEN PRICE, (Pierce?) described in Mass. Archives,
Vol. 45, p. 282, as "of Lebanon; 25 years of age; five feet, eight
inches in stature; light complexion;" engaged to reinforce the Thirteenth Co. of the Second Reg't of the Continental Army for nine
months agreeable to a resolve of the General Court of the State of
Mass. Bay, passed 9 June, 1779. I know nothing more relating to
this man.

Did the roll contain *Price* for *Pierce?* Stephen Pierce who married *Elly* Ricker 7 Feb., 1781, was recorded among the marriages
performed by the Rev. Isaac Hasey.

QUIMBY.

69. DANIEL CLARK QUIMBY, of Lebanon enlisted soon after 14 July, 1776, when "Parson" Hasey recorded : "Bill up by D. Quimby for himself bound into ye army." He was in Capt. John Drew's Co. raised for Canada out of Col. Evans's and Col. Badger's Regt's. His name occurs on a roll dated Charlestown, 27 July, 1776. He resided on Gerrish's Hill on the lot now (1896) owned by Richard H. Goodwin and opposite Charles S. Orrell's house. His wife's name was Betsey, and the First Church records contain baptisms of their children as follows :

i, HANNAH, bapt. 22 March, 1785; m, at Lebanon 9 Aug., 1801, David Hanson.
ii. JOHN, bapt. 22 March, 1785; m. at Lebanon 8 March, 1804, Hannah Hanson.
iii. REBECCA, bapt. 22 March, 1785.
iv. DANIEL, bapt. 6 Nov., 1785; apprenticed as tailor to Daniel Corson: m. 8 Dec., 1800, at Rochester N. H., to Susanna Murray of Farmington, N. H.; removed to Milton, N. H.: but before removing erected the house in Lebanon now (1896) owned by Ellis Hurd: d. in 1856.
v. EDMUND, bapt. 24 Aug., 1788.

RANKINS.

70. JAMES RANKINS, son of John Rankins of Lebanon, enlisted from Lebanon, as a private, early in the Spring 1780 or 1781 for three years in the Fourth Reg't, Mass. line, Col. Sheppard commanding the Regiment and Gen. Henry Knox the Brigade ; he was discharged in 1783. His widow Sarah was a pensioner for many years.

On 29 March, 1786, he married at Lebanon Sarah Champing (Champen) a sister to his brother Jonathan's wife. He removed from Lebanon to West Pond (now Rome), Maine, in 1792, where he resided until his death 22 Nov., 1799. His widow Sarah was living at Lebanon in 1844 at the age of 76 years when she received a bounty for her husband's services from the State under the resolves of 1835-6. She resided with her son Jonathan F. Rankins in Lebanon in 1838. (Land Office, Files, No. 791, Augusta, Maine).

71. JOHN RANKINS of Lebanon enlisted 5 May, 1775, in Capt. Eben'r Sullivan's Co. of the Thirteenth Reg't. of Foot commanded by Col. James Scammon and belonging to the Army of the United Colonies of North America. (Mass. Archives, Vol. 56, p. 201).

As a sergeant of the Mass. line, he was living and receiving a pension in 1820.

On "1 Oct., 1769, John Ranken and Peggy Door were married," by "Parson" Hasey at Lebanon.

72. JONATHAN RANKINS, s. of John and born about 1760, is mentioned in Mass. Archives, vol. 37, p. 108, as "a private belonging to Lebanon in Capt. John Goodwin's Co. in a detachment of militia from the County of York under command of Major Daniel Little-

field on an expedition to Penobscott in compliance with a resolve of the Honorable, the Council of this State [Mass.] passed June ye 29, 1779."

He served two months from 10 July to 10 Sept., 1779; and travelled 210 miles.

He was married at Lebanon 12 March, 1784, to Molly Champen by the Rev. Isaac Hasey who spelled his name Rankens. She was a sister to his brother James's wife. He resided at "Blaisdell's Corner" where he died 6 Feb., 1826, ae. 66 years (g. s.) and lies buried in the First Parish Cemetery.

He had sons Jonathan Jr. and Daniel who lived and died in Lebanon. Jonathan Jr. was b. 9 Oct., 1788; m. at Lebanon, 27 June, 1812, Olive Gubtail (Guptill) of Berwick, Me.; she was b. 26 Oct. 1786.

RICHARDS.

73.   JOHN RICHARDS, Jr., son of John and Abigail (Miles or Myers) Richards of Rochester, N. H., was born in 1754; bapt. at Rochester 14 Apr., 1754.

John, the father, was born in 1722 and removed early to Rochester where 27 June, 1746, he was wounded and captured by the Indians who carried him to Canada.   He was in captivity one year and a half, when he returned to Rochester.   He resided near the center of the town on the lot recently owned by the late Hon. Jacob Hart Ela.   He died in 1792 at the age of 70 years.   Tradition has it that he and the boy named Jonathan, or Philip, Door were taken as far as the "Gully Oven" in Torreow, Leb. ,where they rested on the first night of their capture.

John, the son, enlisted 2 June, 1775, in Capt. Winborn Adams's Co., and is described as "yeoman," aged "25." He was in the battle of Bunker Hill.

He again enlisted in Capt. John Brewster's Co. of Col. Pierce Long's Reg't, stationed at New Castle, N. H., from 7 Aug., 1776, to 7 Jany., 1777. He, with his company, marched to join the northern army in Jan., 1777, and was stationed at Ft. Independence near Ticonderoga.   Here he narrowly escaped capture.   Again he served as a private in Capt. Daniel McDuffee's Co. from 8 Sept. to 15 Dec., 1777.   He marched to Bennington and to Saratoga where he witnessed the surrender of Burgoyne.   He was a miller by occupation, and about 1830 he removed to Lebanon, Me.   He d. at Leb. 7 March, 1834, ae. 80 years (g. s.).   He m. Sarah Bickford by whom he had children as follows :

  i. DAVID, who d. unmarried at the age of 22 years.
  ii. SARAH, bapt. 11 Nov., 1792; m. Jonathan S. Brown.
  iii. SAMUEL, m. Mary Earl.
  iv. JOHN, JR., a clergyman.
  v. ABIGAIL, bapt. 12 Nov., 1792; m. and removed to Ohio, where she d. about 1858.
  vi. ELIZABETH, bapt. 11 Nov., 1792; m, Jonathan Brown: d. at Wakefield, N. H., in 1855.

vii. JAMES, b. 10 Aug., 1791; bapt. 11 Nov., 1792; m. Matilda Merrill(?) clergyman; removed to Ohio in 1813.
viii. LOIS, bapt. "at her own desire," 19 Aug., 1810; d. at Dover, N. H., about 1853.
ix. ABRAM, b. 1795; m. 25 March, 1819, Lovey, dang. of Lieut. Levi and Sally Hodsdon (Corson) of Lebanon; was in the battle of Tippecanoe under Gen. William Henry Harrison in 1811; Methodist clergyman; resided in Lebanon.
x. ISAAC, enlisted in U. S. Army in 1819; never heard from.

ROBERTS.

74.   LOVE ROBERTS, JR., was the son of Love and Mary (Roberts)Roberts.   His father, Love Roberts, Sr., was a son of Thomas Roberts and a grandson of John Roberts, Marshal of the Province of New Hampshire, and Constable at Dover, N. H., in 1679.   He was a great grandson of Thomas Roberts the emigrant, who according to Winthrop was President of the Court, but Belknap makes him Governor of the Province.

Love Roberts, Jr., born in 1745 (or 1752) was residing in Somersworth, N. H., at the beginning of the Revolution.   On 5 May, 1775, he enlisted in Capt. Ebenezer Sullivan's Co. of the Thirteenth Reg't of Foot, commanded by Col. James Scammon.   Capt. Sullivan was of Berwick, Me., and Col. Scammon of Saco, Me.

Mr. Roberts enlisted for the years 1775 and 1776, and was one of the soldiers of Somersworth, N. H., who received an abatement of taxes, 10 Dec., 1776.   For some years before his death, which occurred in Nov., 1841, he resided in Lebanon, Me.; and during his last years, he lived with his son-in-law, Timothy Wentworth, occupying the farm, now (1896) owned and occupied by Gershom Jones in the northerly part of the town.

He married (1) Elizabeth Brown of Epping, N. H., and (2) Betsey, daug. of Benjamin and Dorcas (Ricker) Hersom of L. (38)

Children by wife Elizabeth (Brown) not arranged in order:

i. PAUL, m. Anna Roberts, a cousin.
ii. MARY, (or POLLY) m. Asa Fox.
iii. EZEKIEL, m. Sabra White.
iv. SARAH, (SALLY) m. John Kimball.
v. JAMES, m. Hannah Smith.
vi. HANNAH, m. Wentworth Loud.
vii. LOVE, JR., m. ―― ――
viii. ELIZABETH, (BETSEY) m. Timothy, s. of Amaziah Wentworth of L.

SCATES.

75.   BENJAMIN SCATES of Lebanon, and of Milton, N. H., was living in Lebanon previous to 1775.   He was son of Abigail Scates, who was ill at his house in Lebanon 18 Feb., 1776.   He was a private in Capt. John Goodwin's Co. "in a detachment of militia from the County of York, under command of Major Daniel Littlefield, on an expedition to Penobscott in compliance with a resolve of the Honorable, the Council of this State [Mass.] passed June y⁵ 29, 1779."   He served two months, from 10 July to 10 Sept., 1779, and travelled

two hundred and ten miles. Major Littlefield was of Wells, and Capt. Goodwin of Lebanon. (Mass. Archives, Vol. 37, p. 108.)

He resided in the Salmon Falls river valley on the most westerly farm in town, which he sold to John Cottle of Kittery, the first of the name Cottle to come to town. The farm is now (1896) owned by the heirs of Henry Cottle.

Scates removed to Milton Ridge, N. H. His wife's name was Lydia, and the First Parish records of Lebanon show their children as follows :

  i. Johx. bapt. 7 May, 1775; m. 25 Nov., 1798, Mary Worster of Roch-
    ester, N. H.
  ii. Hanxah. bapt. 28 May, 1780.
  iii. Lucy, bapt. 22 Sept., 1782. m. at Rochester, N. H., 9 May, 1799,
    Richard Horne of Rochester.
  iv. Isaac, bapt. 17 July, 1785.

The following baptisms of children of Benjamin Scates are on Rochester, N. H., First Parish records :

  v. Nortox, bapt. 27 June, 1790; m. at Rochester, N. H., 22 Nov.,
    1812, Hannah Cook of Rochester.
  vi. Benjamix, Jr., bapt. 10 April. 1794; m. at Rochester, 27 Jan.,
    1820, Lovey Lyman, both then of Milton. N. H.

A Lydia Scates m. 15 Nov., 1797, at Rochester, N. H., Frederick Cate of Rochester.

SHERMAN.

76. Thomas Sherman, Sr., son of Anthony and Silence (Ford) Sherman of East Bridgewater, Mass., was born at Rochester, Mass., 18 April, 1754. He was a master mariner in early life. He enlisted as a private 20 Sept., 1776, in Capt. Abram Washburn's Co. of Col. John Cushing's Reg't, and served two months, being stationed at Newport, R. I. He married Betsey Keith, daug. of Daniel and Lydia (Keyzer) Keith, grand daughter of John and Hannah (Washburn) Keith, and great grand daughter of Rev. James and Susanna (Edson) Keith, all of Bridgewater, Mass. (Rev. James Keith was a native of Scotland, educated at Aberdeen, and became the first minister at Bridgewater in 1664, having come to New England two years earlier.) She was born 1 Jan., 1763. He resided in Brookfield, Mass., in 1782; removed to East Bridgewater where he resided from about 1785 to about 1794. He then removed to Tamworth, N. H., where he remained until about 1811. He then removed to Shapleigh, (now Acton) Maine, and about 1814 removed to a border farm between Lebanon and Acton. Here he died 2 Feb., 1846, æ. 92 years (g. s.) ; his wife Betsey died 4 Dec., 1841, æ. 79 years (g. s.) He and his wife became members of the First Orthodox church at Lebanon in March, 1824. Enoch P. Sherman now (1896) owns and occupies their farm.

Mr. Sherman was a direct descendant of William Sherman, the Pilgrim of Plymouth, through Anthony[4]. William[3], William[2], William[1]. William Sherman, the Pilgrim, was in Plymouth as early as 1632, but finally settled in Marshfield, Mass. He married in 1639,

Prudence Hill and had a son William, Jr., who married in 1667, Desire, daughter of Edward and Faith (Clark) Doty, or Doten. This Edward Doty was a "Mayflower" Pilgrim.

William, Jr., and Desire (Doty) Sherman had a son William, born in 1671, who married in 1697, Mercy, daughter of Peregrine and Sarah (Bassett) White. This Peregrine, born in Provincetown Harbor in 1620, was the son of William and Anna, called Susanna, (Fuller) White. This Anna (Fuller) White after the death of her husband William, in 1621, married, second, Edward Winslow, Governor of the Plymouth Colony, and died in Marshfield, Mass., in 1680. It appears, by an examination of Davis's "Ancient Land-Marks of Plymouth," that Thomas Sherman, Sr., was a descendant of Edward Doty, William White and Susanna (Fuller) White of the "Mayflower," and of William Bassett, whose daughter Sarah married Peregrine White, and who came in the "Fortune" in 1621.

Thomas and Betsey (Keith) Sherman had the following children:

    i. ANTHONY, b. Brookfield, Mass., 7 Dec., 1782.
    ii. DANIEL, b. E. Bridgewater, Mass., 7 Jan. 1785.
   iii THOMAS, JR., b. E. Bridgewater, Mass., 30 March, 1787; m. at or near Miramichi. New Brunswick, about 1819, Eleanor Sutherland of Miramichi, New Brunswick; farmer; lived on the Sherman homestead in L.; d. about 1863; she was b. 1 March, 1800, and d. about 1869; ten children.
    iv. JOSEPH KEITH, b. E. Bridgewater, Mass., 12 Dec., 1789.
    v. NATHAN, b. E. Bridgewater, Mass., 7 July, 1792; d. 17 July, 1793
    vi. NATHAN, 2d, b. E. Bridgewater, Mass., 11 May, 1794.
    vii. LYDIA, b. Tamworth, N. H., 3 Dec., 1796.
    viii. NAOMI, b. Tamworth, N. H., 1 May, 1799.
    ix. BETSEY, b. Tamworth, N. H., 8 May, 1802.
    x. HANNAH, b. Tamworth, N. H., 17 Oct., 1806; m. at L. 16 June, 1842, Henry T. Morrill of Lincoln, Me.
    xi. MARTIN W., b. Tamworth, N. H., 20 May, 1810; lived at Emery's Mills, Shapleigh, Me.

STEVENS. (STEPHENS.)

77. BENJAMIN STEVENS (Stephens) was a private in Capt. John Goodwin's Co. "in a detachment of militia from the County of York under command of Major Daniel Littlefield on an expedition to Penobscott in compliance with a resolve of the Honorable, the Council of this State [Mass.] passed June y 29, 1779.

He served two months, from 10 July to 10 Sept., 1779, and travelled 210 miles.

He married at Lebanon 16 March, 1786, Elly or Etty Stanton.

78. JOSEPH STEVENS, born about 1756, enlisted 1 Oct., 1781, in Capt. Joshua Woodman's Co. of Col. Reynold's Reg't of New Hampshire militia.

He re-enlisted from Lebanon 29 March, 1783, as a volunteer substitute for Jonathan Burrows (4) of Lebanon to serve twenty-two months in Capt. Bowman's Co. of the Fifth Mass. Reg't, and received pay for services due Burrows from 15 Jan., 1782.

79. SAMUEL STEVENS is named in Mass. Archives, Vol. 56, p. 196, as "of Lebanon, drummer, enlisted 20 May, 1775, in Capt. Philip Hubbard's Co. of Col. James Scammon's Reg't. Rev. Isaac Hasey wrote 27 May, 1775, "Bill up by Sam Stevens for himself going into ye army."

He was born in 1743, and was living in Lebanon as early as 1773 on the westerly part of the farm now (1896) owned by the heirs of Charles B. Chamberlain. About 1784 he removed to the farm now (1896) owned and occupied by Daniel Stevens. He became a member of the First Church in 1773, and his wife Abigail in 1774. In 1803 he was appointed a deacon in the First Free Baptist church. He d. 26 Dec., 1823, æ. 80 years, (g. s.) and his widow Abigail d. 15 Dec., 1829, æ. 95 years. (g. s.)

Issue by wife Abigail :

    i. DANIEL, bapt.11 July, 1773; m.at L. 26 July, 1795, Judith Ellis; removed to Belgrade, Me.
    ii. ABIGAIL, bapt. 11 July, 1773; m. 3 Oct., 1787, Jeremiah Hill of L.
    iii. SALLY, bapt. 11 July, 1773.
    iv. ABIJAH, bapt. 16 June, 1776.
    v. THOMAS, bapt. 18 Oct., 1778; removed to Belgrade, Me., and later went West.
    vi. MOSES, bapt. 17 Feb., 1782; m. (1) Betsey Scammons who d. 25 Nov., 1819, ae. 36 yrs. (g. s.); m. (2) Nancy Wakenn who d. 1 Aug. 1850, ae. 62 yrs., 2 mo. (g. s.); he d. 27 Dec. 1844, ae. 62 yrs., 3 mo. (g. s.)

80. WILLIAM STEVENS, born at Lebanon in 1753, or 1755, was probably the son of Abijah Stevens, one of the early settlers of Lebanon. He is described on the war rolls as "of Lebanon, husbandman, 20 years of age, in Capt. Jonathan Wentworth's Co.," roll dated 13 June, 1775. He was No. 39 of his Co., and enlisted 30 May, 1775.

I conjecture that he enlisted a second time, for I find on the rolls the name "William Stephenson of Lebanon, a private in a Co. commanded by Capt. Jedediah Goodwin (of Berwick) of Col. Edward Wigglesworth's Reg't; discharged 30 Nov., 1776." This is consistent with the Rev. Isaac Hasey's diary, for 20 Oct., 1776, viz. : "Bill up by Abijah Stevens for a son in ye Army." I know that the war rolls contain many mis-spelled names, and after diligent search I can find no family named Stephenson living in Lebanon before 1800.

William Stevens, however, lived here ; m. Molly Ricker of Lebanon, and removed to Belgrade, Me., about 1796, where he died in 1836, æ. 83 years. His wife Molly died in 1825, æ. 75 years. Their son Daniel was born at Lebanon 30 April, 1784, and died at Belgrade, Me., 18 Aug., 1867. He was the grandfather of Hon. Greenleaf T. Stevens of Augusta, Me.

TEBBETTS.

81 PHILIP TEBBETTS, of Lebanon, enlisted 3 Sept., 1776, as a private in Capt. John Brewster's Co. of Col. Pierce Long's Reg't, sta-

tioned at New Castle, N. H. He was No. 53 and served 95 days
with extra time to 7 Jan., 1777.
He re-enlisted from Lebanon as a private in Capt. Samuel Grant's
Co. of Col. Titcomb's Reg't, and received pay 18 July, 1777, for
services for two months and for travelling *to* and *from* Rhode Island.
He was of Hubbardstown Plantation, Shapleigh, when he m. at
Berwick, Me., 9 May, 1780, Sarah Grant.

WARREN.

82   GEORGE WARREN is named in the Mass. Archives, Vol. 28,
p. 138, as of Lebanon, having enlisted for nine months. He arrived
at headquarters 28 June, 1778.
He was a blacksmith and a resident of Lebanon as early as 1775.
He occupied the lots now (1896) owned and occupied by Alfred
Willey, the heirs of Jonathan Young and the heirs of Daniel W.
Horne, in the westerly part of the town. After a residence of several years he removed from town. His wife's name was Mary, and
the First Parish records show their children as follows :
    i. GEORGE, bapt. 12 Nov., 1776.
    ii. HANNAH HODGSDON, bapt. 12 Nov., 1776.
    iii. BENJAMIN HODGSDON, bapt. 22 March, 1785.

WENTWORTH.

83.   CALEB WENTWORTH, son of Thomas and Mary (Nock) Wentworth was b. 20 Oct., 1754. At the age of 21 he enlisted from
Somersworth, N. H., 26 May, 1775, in Capt. Jonathan Wentworth's
Co., and served two months and nine days. He was then a "joyner,"
enlisted as a private, and was allowed for travelling 74 miles.
Capt. Jonathan Wentworth's Co. was in Col. Enoch Poor's Regt.
After the Revolution he removed to Lebanon where on 15 May,
1780, he married (1) Sarah, daug. of John James, the first of that
name to settle in L. She d. 15 Sept., 1792, æ. about 36 years. He
married (2) Feb., 1799, Mrs. Lydia (Brackett) Stanton, widow of
Benjamin Stanton. He d. at L. 7 April, 1830 ; she d. 24 Jan., 1839,
æ. 73 years, 3 months. He resided on the farm now (1896) owned
and occupied by Samuel Demerritt Hayes at W. Lebanon.
Issue by wife Sarah (James) :
    i. ABRA, b. 10 Apr., 1781; d. single.
    ii. HANNAH, b. 10 Jan., 1783; m. at L. 27 Dec., 1806, Joseph Lord
        who d. 6 Dec., 1866 ae. 85 y., 4 mo.; she d, 15 June, 1835, ae.
        52 y. 5 mo., (g. s.).
    ii. THOMAS, b. 5 Dec., 1784; m. 12 Feb., 1804 Rachel Jones; State
        Rep. in 1839, 1840; selectman Lebanon many years: York Co.
        Commissioner in 1837; d. 14 Feb., 1864.
    iv. LOVEY, b. 19 Nov., 1786; m. at L. 17 Jan., 1805 William McCrellis
        son of Richard and Jane (McCrellis) Furbush of L. He d. at
        L. 4 Dec., 1822; she d. 14 Nov., 1839.
    v. SAMUEL, b. 1 March, 1789; m. 1 Jan., 1818 Rachel daug. of
        Daniel and Lydia (Wentworth) Furbush; he d. 22 Aug., 1857.
Issue by wife Lydia (Brackett-Stanton) :
    vi. SARAH, b. 30 Nov., 1799; d. 12 June, 1804.

vii. Mary, b. in Lebanon 10 June, 1802; m. in 1821 Jotham Winn of Lebanon; she resided on the homestead, and d. 11 Nov., 1869.
viii. BETSY, b. 26 Nov., 1804; m. in Sept. 1828 Elisha son of Samuel Shapleigh by his first wife.
ix. SALLY, b. 1 March, 1807; m. 5 Apr., 1832 Jonathan Blaisdell of Lebanon.

84. JEDEDIAH WENTWORTH, born 2 Nov., 1748, was the son of Thomas and Mary (Knox) Wentworth, of Somersworth, N. H. He enlisted in Capt. Jonathan Wentworth's Co. in 1775; and before the end of his term of service secured a substitute in the person of Jonathan Clark.

He lived in Berwick for a time, but removed to Lebanon previous to 1790. He was a blacksmith and resided on the farm now (1896) owned and occupied by Isaac Chamberlain, which he sold to Amos and Obadiah Chamberlain "lot 27 of the First Division and lot lower No. 7 in the Second Division," 24 March, 1817.

He married (1) 8 Sept., 1771, Eunice Clarke of Berwick; (2) at Lebanon 10 Feb., 1794, Shorey Hodsdon, who died at Lebanon 25 Sept., 1847; he died 9 Oct., 1821.

His children by wife Eunice were:

i. ABIGAIL, m. 28 Aug., 1794, her cousin Peter s. of Ebenezer and Martha (Wentworth) Hanson; d. May 1795.
ii. MERCY, m. 1 Aug., 1803, Enoch Hoyt of Rochester, N. H.
iii. MARY (POLLY), d. in L. unmarried.
iv. JAMES, b. in Berwick, Me., 10 Feb., 1779; m. 11 Nov., 1802, Lydia Pierce; was a deacon; d. in Ossipee, N. H., 31 Dec., 1837.
v. JEDEDIAH Jr., m. (1) 20 Sept., 1808, Betsey Hanson; m. (2) unknown women; m. (3) 1831 Lydia Hersom; d. at Somersworth, N. H., 17 April, 1837.
vi. JOHN, b. 11 Mch., 1783; m. 18 Feb., 1811, Abigail Gerrish of Lebanon; d. 7 Aug., 1859.
vii. EUNICE, m. 23 June, 1816, Samuel Shapleigh of Lebanon; his second wife.
viii. MOSES, b. 8 March, 1788; m. (1) 8 Jan., 1820, Sally Jackson; m. (2) 4 Nov., 1832, Patience daug. of Tobias Smith.
ix. NATHANIEL, b. in Lebanon 10 May, 1790; m. 5 Sept., 1811, Olive Clancey; d. in Denmark, Me., 19 Apr., 1846.

By wife Shorey:

x. ABIGAIL, b. 8 Nov., 1796; m. 2 Feb., 1820, Jonathan Spencer of Berwick, Me.
xi. JOSHUA, b. 2 Sept., 1802; m. 18 Dec., 1823, Esther Perkins.

85. RICHARD WENTWORTH was the son of Thomas and Mary (Knox) Wentworth of Somersworth, N. H.

He was in the Revolutionary army, and received a pension for his services. Congress voted him a bounty of $200 for his gallantry in killing an Indian chief while in the military services.

He resided for many years in Berwick, Me., owning the farm now (1896) owned and occupied by George Knox, Sr.; but in his old age he removed to L., residing with his brother Caleb. He d. at L. 17 June, 1836, æ. 87 (g. s.) Wentworth Genealogy, Vol. 1, p. 390, gives his death 15 June, 1835, æ. 89.

He married Joanna Clark, who received a pension after his death, and d. at L. 28 July, 1838, æ. 86. They had:

. STEPHEN, b. at Berwick, 1767; m. 22 Dec., 1791 Sally Nutter; resided in Ossipee, Moultonboro', and Somersworth, N. H.
ii. RICHARD JR., b. 1769; m. 3 July 1794 Lydia daug. of Jacob Lord; she b. 1775; he soldier in War of 1812.
iii. JOANNA, m. Wentworth son of Benjamin Lord of Berwick, Me
iv. NATHAN, b. 1774; m. Lydia Whitehouse.
v. MARY, b. 1776; d. at age of 21.
vi. RUTH, b. 12 May 1778; m. 15 Nov. 1807 Paul, s. of Samuel Wentworth
vii. THOMAS, b. Berwick, 13 June, 1782; m. Mary Heard.
viii. CALEB. b. 1784; in the War of 1812.
ix. CLARK. b. 4 Apr., 1792; wounded in the battle of Plattsburg.
x. CHARLES, b. 3 Aug., 1794; m. Dec. 1822 Harriet Thompson; resided in Dover, N. H., d. 12 Apr., 1861.

WHITE.

86. JOHN WHITE, supposed son of John and Elizabeth (Cole) White, of Lebanon, settlers on a lot now (1896) owned by James Matthews in the westerly part of the town, and known as the "White field," named in Mass. Archives, Vol. 34, p. 657, as enlisting from Lebanon between 20 Feb. and 10 March, 1777, in Capt. Samuel Derby's Co. of Col. John Bailey's Battalion. He was mustered by Joseph Bragdon of York. He is named as a private of the Mass. line, Revolutionary War, and receiving a pension in 1820. He is said to have removed to Ossipee, N. H.

87. JOSEPH WHITE was a son of John and Elizabeth (Cole) White of Lebanon. He was No. 45 of Capt. Stephen Clark's Co. mustered at Portsmouth, N. H., 21 Nov., 1775. A portion of these troops went to Winter Hill, Charlestown (now Somerville) to take the place of the retiring Conn. troops, in Dec., 1775. He was also in the Fourth Reg't of Patterson's Brigade during the war, as he states in his affidavit.

He married at Lebanon 5 Jan. 1786, Jane, daughter of Lieut. Samuel and Hannah (Hayes) Copp of Lebanon. He removed to Ossipee, N. H., where he was living in 1844, a pensioner of the Federal government.

88. SILAS WHITE, supposed son of John and Elizabeth (Cole) White of Lebanon, enlisted 11 July, 1775, in Capt. Philip Hubbard's Co. of Col. James Scammon's Reg't.

He re-enlisted as a corporal in Capt. John Goodwin's Co. "in a detachment of militia from the County of York under command of Major Daniel Littlefield, on an expedition to Penobscott, in compliance with a resolve of the Honorable, the Council of this State, [Mass.] passed June y^c 29, 1779." He served two months, from 10 July to 10 Sept., 1779, and travelled 210 miles.

He was living in Lebanon in 1767, and raised a barn there 24 Sept., 1784. He married Rachel, daughter of Joseph and Eunice (Shorey) Wentworth. She was born 17 April, 1756. They lived in Lebanon, but removed to Ossipee, N. H. They had nine girls and five boys, but the children's names I no not know.

WHITEHOUSE.

89. JAMES WHITEHOUSE is named in Mass. Archives. Vol. 56, p. 201, as "of Lebanon; enlisted 5 May, 1775, in Capt. Eben'r Sullivan's Co. of the Thirteenth Reg't of Foot, commanded by Col. James Scammon and belonging to the Army of the United Colonies of North America.

He was married at Lebanon 19 Dec., 1776, to Mary Door by "Parson" Hasey. A family of this surname lived in Lebanon on the "Plains," near Berwick line in early times.

WINGATE.

90. ENOCH WINGATE, a native of Rochester, N. H., and son of Benjamin or Samuel Wingate of Rochester, was in the army in 1778. The Rev. Isaac Hasey wrote in his diary 29 Nov., 1778: "Bill of thanks by Wingate for his sons returned from ye Army." I have no proof that he ever lived in Lebanon, but he and the Wingate family were attendants at Mr. Hasey's church. He probably lived near "Adams's Corner" in Rochester, N. H.

WITHERELL.

91. JAMES WITHERELL, born 24 Nov., 1755, was a brother to Thomas Witherell, Jr., one of the early settlers of Lebanon; also brother to John (92). He came to this town as early as 1775.

He enlisted as a private 22 July, 1776, in a company commanded by Capt. Jedediah Goodwin of Berwick, of Col. Edward Wigglesworth's Reg't; and was discharged at Albany, N. Y., 30 Nov., 1776. His company set out for Canada, according to "Parson" Hasey.

On 1 Aug., 1776, Mr. Hasey wrote in his diary: "Bill up by Tom Witherell for a son in ye army." This seems to show that his father was Thomas, unless his brother Thomas had a son then in the army.

James, the soldier, was a tavern-keeper in the westerly part of the town on the farm now (1896) owned and occupied by Daniel Grant. He sold his property to Jonathan Y. Wentworth and removed to Monmouth, Me. He married at Lebanon 17 April, 1781, Martha, daughter of John Gerrish of Berwick Me.; she was born 9 Sept,, 1760.

Mr. Witherell was town clerk in 1787 and 1788, and the third representative to the General Court in 1795.

His children by wife Martha were:

    i. ISAAC, b. 16 Sept., 1782; bapt. 22 Aug., 1790.
    ii. ADAH, b. 21 Jany., 1786; bapt. 22 Aug., 1790.
    iii. SOPHIA, bapt. 22 Aug., 1790.
    iv. JOHN KENNEY, bapt. 6 March, 1791.

91. JOHN WITHERELL, a brother of James (91) and of Thomas Witherell, Jr., an early settler of Lebanon, was a sergeant in Capt. John Goodwin's Co. "in a detachment of militia from the County of York, under command of Major Daniel Littlefield, on an expedition

48

to Penobscot, in compliance with a resolve of the Honorable, the Council of this State [Mass.] passed June y⁰ 29, 1779."

 _ His wife was Mary Morrill, daughter of John Gerrish of Berwick, and the following children I find named on the First Church records :

    i. NELLY, bapt. 17 Sept., 1780.
    ii. ELIZABETH, bapt. 10 Jany., 1781.
    iii. MARY MORRILL, bapt. 26 Aug., 1782.
    iv. MARTHA. bapt. 6 June, 1790.

He had a son William who resided in Monmouth, Me., where I conjecture the whole family resided after living in Lebanon for several years.

He married at Berwick, Me., 28 March, 1778, Mary Morrill Gerrish.

YOUNG.

93. ABNER YOUNG enlisted from Lebanon as a private, 3 Sept., 1776, in Capt. John Brewster's Co. of Col. Pierce Long's Reg't, stationed at New Castle, N. H. He was No. 55 and served until 7 Jan., 1777.

94. JOHN YOUNG enlisted from Lebanon as a private 24 Sept., 1776, in Capt. Abraham Perkins's Co. of Col. Pierce Long's Reg't, stationed at New Castle, N. H. He received one month's advanced pay from 7 Jan., 1777, but when ordered to march to Ticonderoga on 13 Jan., 1777, he refused, claiming that as he was a citizen of Mass., he was not bound by the military orders of New Hampshire. He resided in the southern part of the town. A Jno. Young died of nervous fever 3 Sept., 1785, according to Mr. Hasey's diary for 1785.

95. JONATHAN YOUNG is named on War Rolls, Mass. Archives, Vol. 43, p. 94, as of Lebanon; mustered between 30 May and 13 June, 1777, in Capt. Samuel Derby's Co. of Col. John Bailey's Battalion. He was mustered by Joseph Bragdon of York.

www.ingramcontent.com/pod-product-compliance
Lightning Source LLC
Chambersburg PA
CBHW021554270326
41931CB00009B/1213